Cancer Moon

How I Survived the
Best Years of My Life

JENNA TICO

SHE WRITES PRESS

Published 2024
Printed in the United States of America
Print ISBN: 978-1-64742-762-7
E-ISBN: 978-1-64742-763-4
Library of Congress Control Number: [LOCCN]

For information, address:
She Writes Press
1569 Solano Ave #546
Berkeley, CA 94707

Interior Design by Tabitha Lahr

She Writes Press is a division of SparkPoint Studio, LLC.

For the ones who feel it all.

Born with the moon in Cancer,
give her a name she will answer to.
—Joni Mitchell

Through dangers untold and hardships
unnumbered, I have fought my way here . . .
to take back the child you have stolen, for
my will is as strong as yours and my kingdom
as great. You have no power over me!
—Jennifer Connelly, *Labyrinth* (1986)

Jenna, you're a lot of car.
—Isabel Nelson, senior year of high school

Contents

Come Sit in the Palm of My Hand

*A*nd take a rest for a while. It's been a long life getting here, which I know, because I am here too. Take a beat. Try and relax. Or don't try, and see what happens.

Don't get too caught up in what any of this means, or whether I've exaggerated, or if I've changed the names of those involved. Because I have and also haven't. I don't know if this is poetry or prose, in the same way I don't know if I'm old or young. Do you?

Life is nuanced, truly, and stranger than anything I could invent here in these pages, so I haven't bothered. Instead, I've tried to be kind; to myself, mostly, and to the memories committed here to word. What follows represents the years of my life between twenty and thirty. I was on my way to becoming a partner, a mother, and a decent human being, with something resembling self-esteem, but not at all there yet. People (who are these people? I'd like to meet them, and maybe accidentally-on-purpose spill hot coffee on their shoes) often describe the twenties as the "best years of your life," but I found them to be a bit like doing a cartwheel on top of a moving vehicle, while also trying to suck in my stomach and wondering if it's too late to take Plan B. I also spent most of that decade being told I was too much, or pining after ~~stunted~~ unavailable men, or trying not to cry on public transportation, when it even existed. I live in Southern California, so I more often tried not to cry while riding a borrowed bicycle or coasting my 1,000-year-old Toyota Camry down a hill on $5 worth of gas.

For me, the twenties represented phases of the moon: the only constant being change and the amount of light visible. At the start, I waned—shrinking away from the person I'd constructed to survive childhood and launching straight into an ego death, or whatever you want to call the time when we feel the compulsive need to cut our own bangs and bang people who make us feel shitty about ourselves.[1] After that ran its course, I went fully dark—at least to the naked eye—in the shadow of partners who had not tackled their pain and, in my survival, became new. Then I grew: and I don't want to give anything away, but a big part of that growth had to do with finally being cool with the women in my genetic line. I stopped blaming others, and claimed my life. Before long (but what felt like a gazillion years) I was full: of joy, reflection, sometimes crap, sometimes myself, and then eventually another whole human being. That human being is almost in preschool now, and we are both very sleepy. (Okay, mostly me.)

I have always been one with big feelings. In 2000, I was the only one in the whole fifth-grade class who voted for Ralph Nader in the mock Presidential election, simply because I intuitively felt he needed more love.[2] As a teen, I invited my friend Nate to the King of Hearts dance, a Sadie Hawkins-esque experiment interesting in principle but utterly stupid in implementation (much like high school). I made this choice despite my better judgment and despite the quite obvious fact Nate loved my friend, Elena. But wait—he listened to Death Cab for Cutie! Once, while reading a vulnerable poem in front of my English

---

1. Maybe you never did that? If so, good for you. No, seriously. Do a TED talk.
2. This inspired a kid named Max to harass me for the remainder of the year, saying "Jenna! Nader ONE" while holding up a solitary index finger and laughing maniacally. Naturally, I pledged to marry him.

class, I watched as a solitary tear slipped from his eye and tracked down his cheek. Soulmates!!! After the dance, and after watching pathetically on as Nate and Elena danced to "Get Low" for three hours straight, I was wracked with angst, if not surprise. While sitting on the steps, my best friend, Isabel—already an anthropologist of my moods—placed her arm around my shoulders.

"Why?" I asked her, a solitary tear slipping from my eye. "Is there something wrong with me?"

She paused, before finally answering. "There's nothing wrong with you. He just can't handle you. Jenna . . . you're a lot of car."

It took approximately fifteen years, many more tears, and many more moons to recognize that Isabel had given me the best compliment of my life.

I've always been a lot of car. Astrologically speaking, I'm a Cancer moon, and only just realized not everyone ugly cries at the opening notes of *The Lion King*. I spent much of my early adulthood trying (in vain) to hide my sensitivity, which resulted in bubbling up and mass explosion all over whomever happened to meet me in the 2010s. I could say I regret nothing, and that is probably true. But, I also know more now and have more love for the squishy parts of myself living under the rock. They are important, too.

Making sense of my experience in retrospect—usually late in the night—was an essential part of the treacherous and beautiful terrain of growing up; of falling in love and getting ghosted, sometimes in the same day; of finally saying NO to men who kissed me in the dark but "oopsie, have a girlfriend!"; of pulling above the waterline of emotionally abusive relationships and ultimately meeting my life's true partner, who is now my husband. He looks good in almost EVERY SHADE OF YELLOW, which doesn't make sense, and is almost impossible to freak out (believe me, I've tried). And that kid I mentioned, who is almost in preschool—we made him together. Pretty cool, right?

Life is nuanced. I collected these pieces, many written in my early twenties, and decided not to fuck with them too much. I accept them as they are, not for what I wish they were. I kept many in the present tense, because the woman who wrote each one is still alive within me—and she is a gift. Even when I no longer agree with what she has to say, the woman who believed she had to keep an eyelash curler in the pocket of her pajamas (for the morning after, obvs) is as real as the one who sits here now, barely willing to use a hairbrush.

I remember her.

Anything more current I've managed to get out by freeing myself from the tragic myth of perfectionism, by engineering an escape hatch from the Desire to Sound Important™ and bribing myself with Oreos at odd hours of the day. Recently, I also had to subject my toddler to 10,000 hours of *Daniel Tiger's Neighborhood* so that I could hide in the closet and proofread. I also had to admit, at thirty-two, it is probably too late for me to become a child prodigy. What a fucking relief.

It might be too late for you, too, and that's okay. It's not too late for any of us, though, when it comes to making art out of what we have learned. You are exactly on time to your life. I am happy you are here. It makes sense and also not at all.

Take a rest. I believe the best years of our lives are the ones still ahead or perhaps (squee!) right where we are—having learned enough about ourselves to laugh at the fallout, to wear comfortable shoes, and stop sending questionable texts after 11:00 p.m.

It is so, so vulnerable to love this much. Loving takes a lot of courage.

Courage requires a lot of rest.

You're doing it.

Keep going.

PART I:

Waning

Cabo is the New Cabo

THURSDAY

I'm sitting on the toilet in a stranger's house, surrounded by bottles of corroded nail polish, and wondering if it's too late to say I'm allergic to boats. I snap a selfie, black leggings around my ankles, and send the photo to my boyfriend: "If I die on this trip, remember me like this. And take care of the cat."

I get up, smoothing a panty liner into king-sized under-pants, and lather my hands with TJ Maxx soap. Somewhere, a tiny part of me remembers: I CHOSE to be here. I even squirreled away twenty-dollar bills into an envelope marked "healthy risks!!" like a delusional vision board junkie; just waiting to use that hard-earned cash to be miserable in a bathroom on the way to be miserable on a houseboat in Lake Havasu, Arizona. In case you haven't tried before, Google searching "Lake Havasu" brings up a series of photos featuring the cast of *Deliverance* in ill-fitting bikinis; as the cursor blinks, "Lake+Havasu+Nipple+Tassels" auto fills as the next logical thing to type. Which I did not need my computer to store. Its already doomed algorithm now consists of Lake Havasu, WebMD ("Tiny mark on forehead skin cancer or pimple"; "How old is too old to get pimples"; "Can you die from a UTI") and vacation rentals in Crete—for my vision board, obviously. I may be delusional, but I'm not stupid.

I emerge into the kitchen to find a wilting, three-foot, inflatable penis adorning the counter, propped lovingly amongst a pile of dilapidated pornographic playing cards. Through the creased images, I can make out a smattering of boners—all shades, from milky white to caramel colored! DIVERSITY!—attached to hairless man-boys who lean awkwardly against fences and piles of hay; who sometimes sprawl on blankets that should have borne a picnic, as if to say, *Hey girl, I just happened to be here. Oh what, this erection? I haven't seen that thing since the last time I masturbated under a pile of old t-shirts. But since it's here. . . .*

Above the boners, a string of crooked letters reads "LET'S GET NAUTI" over a dim spread of olive pizza and warm Prosecco. My stepsister's voice breaks through the din of reggae music. "Wait—this is a *nautical* theme?" she shouts, clutching an alcoholic seltzer.

It is 3:30 p.m., and we are about to leave for a three-day bachelorette party. My stepsister, Kate, is thirty-five years old, with an intolerance for bullshit that has eliminated virtually all potential life partners until now. She has lived the past ten of her adult years in San Diego, slowly ascending from tequila brunches to Farmer's Market Sundays; her now-fiancée, John, is a nurse. Vegetarian. Knows how to play poker and would probably brake for an opossum to cross the road. He asked her father for permission to marry Kate and works graveyard shifts when he needs to.

Kate and John kissed with tongue for the first time on Fourth of July five years ago, probably drinking American beer; and he is currently on his way over to deliver a cardboard box of whatever store-brand alcohol the Bachelorette Overlords have decided will get us drunk in the van, on our way to spend an entire weekend getting drunk on a lake.

John, a seasoned handler at this point, is fresh off of his own bachelor party, wherein he and four friends fled to the mountains and nibbled on psychedelic mushrooms for two days before returning home safely, with almost no one puking in the woods. Their mayhem was just enough to skirt the edge, but not too much. Never too much. Just enough to be different, maybe, than the ones who got strippers in Reno.

"Kate—DUH, yes," squeals one of the blondes. Cassie. "I can't believe you just asked that. You guys—I can't believe she just asked that!"

Maybe you already know this? But as I found out, bachelorette parties are a thinly veiled excuse for the bride's unmarried pals to micromanage their closest friends for one entire weekend while getting as hammered as possible. And yes, some people do it differently; but those people do NOT follow Cassie on Instagram, so who cares about them anyway?

Cassie has painstakingly organized each detail of Kate's party, from the matching black bathing suits we all have to wear ("Because won't it look SO CUTE if we're all wearing black, and the bride is wearing white? You guys, won't it? WON'T IT?"), to the tiny bags of plasticky swag waiting for us on the counter, fighting against the sagging pornography for the title of Most Depressing Thing Ever.

Two weeks prior, I had responded to the email about the BLACK BIKINIS, SO CUTE! with something along the lines of: "Great! I'll be the one in the oversized onesie, showing nothing but the small oval of my face." I waited, smug, for the branch of friendship—Aren't we so ridiculous? Isn't life so ridiculous?—to extend across cyberspace but was met instead with a lot of silence and several private responses of, "My friend has a black bikini. Want me to see if you can borrow it?" and "I hear they have super cheap ones at Target."

The swag is chapstick, sunscreen, Advil. Heart-shaped sunglasses in Easter Egg colors. I open my bag, pop an apple-flavored Jolly Rancher into my mouth, and try to remember what Kate said as we ate what I now refer to as the Last Supper on our way to meet the rest of the girls. "They just don't get your sense of *humor*," she laughed, her dimples practically singing as she tapped her hands on the wheel. "It'll get better."

It doesn't.

I want to drink something, anything, to fit in; but beer makes me gassy, and the seltzer smells like eggs. I pick up a red Solo cup. Water?

No. Vodka.

"Everyone look out, Rilo is here!" Cassie's sister, Jules, is sitting in the corner. On a good day, Jules weighs one hundred pounds; today, she is probably ninety-five, just over five feet tall, and holding a bong that is easily six. Next to her, another friend—Lauren—balances a can of beer on the lip of her knee, maneuvering a breast pump with the other. She'd be over with the others, talking and smoking, but she needs to stay plugged into the wall.

"Oh—RILO!" she exclaims, greeting the woman who has just walked into the room. Rilo, graciously accepting a shot of something that might be Listerine, places a platter next to the now completely deflated boner.

"Behold—Kate's brownie!" she presents, proudly.

Lifting the cover off, the gaggle lets out a collective shriek. The brownie is in the shape of yet another penis, crusted with chocolate frosting, looking somewhat diseased, and just waiting to be devoured.

⌒

"Ok, so what I'm *saying* is that you don't just have to go to Mexico to party. Where we're going is—like—a party epicenter. I'm just saying—Lake Havasu is what's up. Lake Havasu is the new Cabo."

We're two hours into a six-hour ride from San Diego to the town outside Lake Havasu, where we have rented four rooms in a Quality Inn that—from the website—looks like the site of at least several crystal-meth-related murders.

In the weeks leading up to the trip communication was impeccable; but now that we are actually inside the van, with an actual human being hitting the gas pedal ("THANK YOU, DANIELLE! OUR DESIGNATED DRIVER! WE LOVE YOU, DANIELLE!!") and a dozen others crammed in, it is clear there is no one in charge. It is anarchy.

One woman sits in the middle, drinking Chardonnay straight from the bottle, trying to dredge up embarrassing memories of Kate. At least three are talking about breastfeeding, and the others are passing around a six pack of Smirnoff Ice, letting pistachio shells fall to the floor mats as they dig through their bags for cell phones, lipstick, gum.

We've already stopped twice; once for peeing on the side of the road and once for "pumping and dumping," where the tipsy mothers of adorably Instagrammed newborns take a moment to commiserate about nipple chafing. The rest of us peruse a Casino convenience store for beer and two-for-one bags of Fritos. We get back in the car, some already needing to pee again, and resume our drive straight into the mouth of hell.

"Just think of the BEST memory you have of Kate," slurs a voice from the back. I think to myself. *The time our parents told us they were getting married, and I made myself cry, just because I knew I had their attention and I wanted them to know how terribly dramatic this all was.*

Kate had been sitting in the corner, sucking on the tip of a bitten down nail, staring at me with that teenage slit-eye that is at once isolating and thrilling. The corners of her mouth twitched up into a smile, knowing, and I suddenly got it: *sisters.* A sister who once detailed the entire plot of *Coyote Ugly* from start to finish, even though I didn't really know what sex was yet. Who taught by example what it meant to say "BUH-BYE" to an endless parade of Maybes; or any man who made her feel anything less than smart, capable, wanted. She is able to jump on the bed and sing any lyric from Destiny's Child, and also a lifeguard who is able to rescue a flailing civilian from drowning in a pool. Strong. Beautiful. Both.

I look down at my phone. My boyfriend has finally texted me back: *Brutal,* he offers, like a man who has never had to watch someone pump breast milk in a Texaco. *Hang in there! I love you.* I feel the familiar coil of belonging shoot up through my stomach, yet pause on something colder, harder: *Most of these women are married,* I think. *Why does that automatically mean that they've won?*

"I'm thinking of the time we blacked out on the party bus and had to jump off the roof the next morning and almost died. Kate! Do you remember? And then we went and got mimosas."

I stare out the window of the moving vehicle I now share with twelve of the most dangerous humans who have ever walked the earth. We finally arrive at the motel, settling into our respective rooms; my new roommate, who loves me with a fierce adoration that can only be produced by off-brand liquor, clutches at my arm with nails longer than her nose. "All I'm saying is she may be my sister-in-law . . ." thick, gravelly, Jersey accent, dramatic pause for emphasis, "but I wouldn't spit on her if she was on fire."

A knock at the door and Cassie arrives in a cloud of Tommy Girl perfume, wearing a shirt that could double as a piñata blindfold for a very small child. "Anyone wanna go out?"

It's 12:30 a.m. in Arizona. The closest source of entertainment is a 7-11, and it's four miles away. I locate my earplugs. The night is young.

To prepare for the trip, I asked my friends point-blank: "Does anyone know of a book that makes you forget where you are the entire time you're reading it?"

So on the second day of Bachelorette Bonanza, I emerge from the hotel room clutching an Irish detective novel—one wary eye open, like a squirrel skidding across a power line—and go into the hotel lobby, which also doubles as the dining room and entertainment center. Tiffany, my Jersey roommate, argues with the concierge/janitor/head chef/CEO about our room charges, and the rest of the crew—bedraggled, but wearing mascara—sit around a linoleum table, discussing true crime.

"All I'm saying is I'm surprised everyone in the '70s wasn't a serial killer." Amanda looks up at the television, a dribble of low-fat milk escaping from her mouth. "It was just so easy. Ted Bundy was in the, like, triple digits or something."

The rest of the crew nods in solemn, hung-over agreement. Cassie begins counting off heads like a deranged carpool mom and beckons for each of us to get into the van. We arrive at the dock nearly two hours, one winding road, and three sing-a-longs of "What's Up" by 4 Non Blondes later; as we stream out of the car, a motley crew of bra adjustments and sunglass selfies, she gathers us close for the lowdown.

"So," Cassie whispers. "The deal is, the boat technically is only supposed to host ten— and there are thirteen of us. So we have to keep things . . . on the down-low."

"WHAT," Rilo retorts, doubling a scrunchie around her cascade of black hair, drowning out the chatter of concern over available bathroom mirrors. "Are you telling me that some of us don't have places to sleep?"

"You can sleep on the roof," Cassie replies, eyeing two men sauntering across the parking lot to meet us. "It'll be super beautiful, under the stars and shit."

"I'll sleep on the roof," I volunteer, imagining the alternative as something akin to taking a red-eye flight with an infant. A drunk infant. "I don't mind."

"But didn't you tell us not to bring blankets?" Annie speaks up from the back of the crowd, lowering her sunglasses to assess the lineup of houseboats bobbing like sad corks against the rock wall. "Because they would take up too much room in the van?"

"Well . . . yes," Cassie replies, voice low. "But we'll figure something out. Dana brought an air mattress. And I have a super-warm hoodie you can borrow."

The concern over Mattress Gate is short-lived, as most people are still too hungover to process the concept of personal space, and the men—who have now identified themselves as our captains—have arrived. Now, I'm not a sailor. The one time I accompanied a friend to Catalina Island, I fell asleep on the deck and spent the rest of the week nursing a horrendous sunburn on my inner thigh. That said, I have a hard time believing any human would assess the two men in front of us and exclaim with conviction: "Yes! I trust these children-men with the precious cargo of my life and to operate heavy machinery upon a large body of water."

The first man, just clearing five-foot-three, immediately identifies himself as a water-skier. One eye is glued shut in what could be leftover sleep granules, but could also be pink eye. The other, nearly his opposite in stature—over six feet tall, probably 140 pounds—has dirt-blond hair pulled into a greasy ponytail, looks very excited to graduate high school one day, and smells of rancid fast food. His wrinkled T-shirt spells out "I Heart Motorboating" in white block letters. I recall the morning's conversation about serial killers and feel my stomach pang in a tragic combination of pity and terror.

Cassie addresses the group. "Shall we get onboard? And decide who is going to go to the store to get supplies?"

Fast forward about twenty-five minutes, after thirteen educated women attempt the near-impossible task of deciding on a grocery list. I watch as the elementary-school teacher in the bunch, now two Tecates deep, takes a show of hands for each preferred type of alcohol.

"I have four people for vodka, ten for beer, six for hard cider, and—Annie! Annie, you've raised your hand for every single one!"

"What?" Annie asks, tugging a curl in one hand. "I like variety."

Meanwhile, the token attorney speaks up from the crowd. "Just get me six bottles of Chardonnay. If anyone else wants wine, get it separately."

Thirty minutes later, I'm walking down the freezing-cold aisles of an Arizona grocery store. "Boxed pizza, ham slices, coffee, salsa . . ." Tiffany pushes the cart with one hand, using the other as an at-the-ready camera, should the perfect moment arise.

"I'm getting tequila," Dana enters, clutching a bottle of expensive Añejo to her chest. "No one raised their hand for tequila. I'm going to sip it throughout the weekend."

We nod in agreement and my cell phone buzzes. "Hello?" I answer, praying it is a good friend who found herself surprisingly close to Arizona. With a private jet.

"Hi!" Kate's voice, rising against a background of cackling laughter and Kendrick Lamar. "Hey—while you're at the store, can you also get Band-Aids?"

"Bitch, who is *bleeding* already?" Tiffany grabs the phone, jabbing at the speakerphone button.

"It's no big deal. Cassie just cut her hand open, and it won't stop bleeding. Speaking of bleeding—can you grab tampons?"

Several hundred dollars and approximately fifty plastic bags later, we are loading our kill into the back of the van. "It's a good thing we are in Arizona," Dana mutters, eyeing the pile of reusable bags we brought but failed to use. "They don't care about the environment here." I stare at the canvas bags stagnating in the trunk. Much like my hopes for the weekend; useful, but left behind. Neglected in favor of convenience.

It's worth noting that even on my best day, I am a hot-and-cold socializer. Some days I am the center of the circle: I will choose the song on the jukebox, this sequined shirt has never looked better, I have the funniest story, I will have another glass. Other days my tragic Irish-American streak takes over, and I'd gladly go on a brooding walk uphill in the snow than speak to even one more human being.

In this moment, and most that followed, I planted myself firmly in the latter; bags of other people's booze slung from each arm, uterus cramping, shoulders already an alarming shade of pink. Everyone already has someone to laugh with. Everyone already has an inside joke. Everyone seems to enjoy the sensation of picking too-small bathing suits out of their butt cracks, cracking open pissy beer, and arguing about Ariana Grande.

I, on the other hand, am more concerned with adjusting the crooked "Let's Get Nauti" sign hanging—annoyingly askew—over the main window than I am with hearing another high-stakes update of *Real Housewives*. I pop a Dramamine, and my stomach churns in obligatory concern.

We begin unloading groceries. "Have a beer," Cassie instructs, exploding the deli supplies onto the counter in a colorful pile of turkey flesh and iceberg lettuce. The women descend upon the wreckage in a way that can only be described as carnal, and I walk to the lip of the boat.

Over the course of the trip, I will come to realize I am the only one concerned with preparing food; later on, after the boat has crashed into our first destination with such violence my sunglasses fly off my face ("that's NORMAL," teenage-captain informs us, picking at a zit on his chin), I timidly broach the subject of dinner. We intended to use the barbecue that night; but the sun, delightfully and ominously pink, is slipping beneath the horizon. The bugs are starting to come out.

I walk over to shore, where Chardonnay Attorney—in nothing but a bikini—teeters along the rocky coast. "I'm gathering *firewood*," she informs me, though neither one of us knows what for. In a flash, I imagine the entire coastline erupting in flame and think of how we will always be known as the ones who destroyed the New Cabo; I cry as I cling to my inflatable mattress, the one thing I've been promised, and hope my bleeding vagina doesn't attract any freshwater sharks or evil spirits or whatever other horrific shit has chosen this lake as its obvious and permanent home.

The fantasy pops, and I step back onto the boat; much to my surprise and relief, I see that Jules has opened the grill. She has that look—the one that people get when they have achieved the perfect combination of marijuana and alcohol to eliminate normal movement—and holds half an onion in one hand. In the other, half a lemon. As I get closer, I see she is rubbing them—obsessively, slowly, like one might pet an elderly cat—onto the grill in order to clean it.

"Does that work?" I ask, watching intently as the lemon juice squirts into her cleavage, but the grill continues its astonishing resemblance to the underwater *Titanic*.

"Don't worry," she says. "My hubby is a chef." He is a bartender.

She attempts a gloppy wink, and the other eye closes as well. I assume this will not only be the night I survive a great fire but also consume raw meat that has been briefly transformed by rusted, lemony metal.

In the space of thirty minutes, dinner is over. The women plunge into the piles of unevenly-cooked meat and Wonder Bread buns and occasionally ask important questions: *Is this vegan? Did you get me the pickles I wanted? Do you want to do another shot?*

Out of the chaos, Cassie emerges into the living room holding a cell phone in one hand and an Apple TV remote in the other. "Ladies," she purrs, "it's that point in the evening where we get to find out just how well the groom knows our bride." Cackles, shouting ensues. Annie is still passed out on the pleather couch, where she has been since 3:00 p.m.

"Jules—cue the video!"

Kate, meanwhile—who is drunk enough to be shouting, but not too drunk to mistake what is happening for anything good—yells for our attention. "LADIES," she asks, pulling a crocheted cover-up over her freckled shoulders. "Is this what I think it is?"

Oh, it is: the *Lord of the Flies* shit these women instigate each time one of them gets married. Months prior, Jules's husband had gotten Kate's soon-to-be-groom blisteringly drunk, asking him a series of questions that—if answered correctly—would determine whether they are Meant. To. Be. No one really discusses what will happen if he gets the questions wrong. Jules stumbles to start the video, immediately hits pause, and clears her throat.

"Ahem. Kate, we will ask you a question, and then see if your answer matches John's. So—what is your favorite book?"

Nervous chatter. "That's easy," Kate replies, adjusting her captain's hat. Did I mention she has a captain's hat?

"Anyone who knows me knows I don't have a favorite book. I have a million favorite books. I honestly could never pick."

Jules hits PLAY. A tiny, pixelated John takes up the screen, face ruddy from drink.

"That's easy," John replies to the same question. "Kate's

favorite book is *A Wrinkle in Time.*" Arms fold, mouth curls up into a smile.

There is a brief pause, and the women erupt into laughter.

"WHAT," Kate squeals. "I mean . . . I read it. Once. In middle school. Jesus, that was stupid."

The rest is a blur. Meaning: the rest of the questions are answered in similar fashion—John, confident as a quarterback, answering one-thousand percent wrong—with Kate taking a shot each time he misses. The group gets louder, bits of burger flying from their hands as they squeal and high five. Around midnight, New Jersey Tiffany emerges from one of the dens, her caramel skin creased from sleep, and rubs the crumbled mascara from her cheek. She observes the carnage. "What are we drinking?"

⌒

"Jesus, Cassie, *lower your voice.* Doesn't your head hurt?"

"No," Cassie answers, peeling a sequined bikini from between her butt cheeks. "I told you. I don't get hung-over."

At the start of the trip, if you'd asked me what my most embarrassing outfit would be, I'd have said the turtleneck-and-cargo-short combo was a shoe-in. No one else brought anything with sleeves, let alone utility pockets and an emergency book light. Fast forward two days: I am sitting on the jutted-out balcony of the houseboat, sun-screened legs mashed into the tanned flesh of at least four other women, and realizing that *this* is it. The black bathing suit photoshoot.

Kate is in the front, still a little drunk, with her captain's hat proudly askew. To the left, the forgotten porno playing cards sit rotting beneath a fine layer of overnight mist, sunscreen, and spilled beer. Out of the sea of bikinis, breasts, and strategic patches of crochet, I look down at the massive black one-piece I borrowed from my aunt; serving the dual function of sheltering my near-translucent skin *and* transporting me back to the unmistakable feeling of seventh grade. Back then, I not only had the wrong body, friends, and favorite movies. I also had the wrong sweatshirt.

I smile anyway, squinting against the unflinching Arizona sun as our child-captain teeters on a rock on the other side of the bow. Earlier that day, when most people still resembled half-drunk wooden soldiers—limbs stiff as they sifted through the massacre of cans, hoping for a flat Red Bull—we began our first official cruise over the lake. And at this point, I will admit, my heart softened. The thick panoply of rocks bracketing the sides of Lake Havasu sat red and proud, shifting colors as the sun moved and sprouting tufts of cacti and birdsong in unexpected pockets, like happy secrets.

I stared out over the water and accepted a cup of something carbonated and alcoholic and began chatting with some of the women about their children, homes, jobs. I saw cracks in the veneer of what I had previously labeled as impenetrable and even began to appreciate our personalized plastic tumblers. I haven't had anything plastic with my name on it since the fifth grade, and even then it was just a cubby, and even then I knew I was supposed to feel too old for that sort of thing. Suddenly, Lauren popped her head up over the staircase, bursting my reverie.

"Hey! The boys are playing video games. You seem like the most responsible person. Do you know how to dock a boat?"

Forty minutes later, we are here: flesh sticking to the hot, plastic, upstairs deck, waiting for someone to snap a group photo. The boat did in fact get docked, though not at my hand; I watched in terrified silence as Amber, a bottle deep in Chard, leapt toward the sand with a rope in her hand, resembling a tiny, shocked spider monkey.

"She was actually a professional wakeboarder at one point," Danielle told me, leaning over the railing. "I know; I was surprised too."

We sit next to each other now, Danielle and I, waiting for the photo spectacle to be over. I have grown fond of her over the course of our two conversations and found solace in the fact she also appears to require things like hand soap, and toast.

She was recently married after being in a relationship with the same man, her now-husband, for ten years; I looked at the tiny row of garnets shimmering on her left ring finger and did not consider what it might have been like for her—just a year prior—to have still been the person without the ring. Without the "in." Without the anchor to cast down at the end of a long day, letting her know that at least—though the boat is bobbing and littered with strays—there's something hitting the ground below. Something to hold on to when you wake in the night, and, in the temporary crazy that sleep creates, you have forgotten where you are.

The captain, who has an iPhone in each hand and at least two tucked under his chin, is desperately trying to please the angry, photogenic mob. "Just turn it a little to the left—no, not like that, no—horizontal! Horizontal, Kevin."

"You can tell he doesn't have a girlfriend," Cassie scoffs, flipping her curtain of blond hair over the opposite shoulder. "Because he hasn't been trained."

We go on like this for half an hour. The only thing that really compares is the pain of having prom photos taken: a dozen teenagers in line like lambs for the slaughter, wilted pink roses adorning tiny wrists as they balance dead-fish hands upon the hips of the person in front of them. All turned to the same side, identical orthodontized smiles, worrying about what part of their baby fat is still sticking out of the place where they shoved it into spandex. This was just like that, only worse, because at least back then I didn't have pubic hair showing. I grin for the camera, my giant safari hat just barely clearing the teeth of the woman behind me.

"It's all for me," Kate says, looking back at her legion of *Heathers*. "All of it."

⌒

There comes a point where one has to wonder how they have survived this long. The lot of them, bikinied and blitzed out of their minds, are also the most entertaining, honest, and disturbingly well-read women to ever enter a room. They feed children out of their bodies and make six figures at work and have definitely, at least once, changed a tire. But the thing is, when thirty-somethings are finally given a weekend away from their toddlers, they almost immediately become toddlers themselves.

For starters, they leave their drinks everywhere. Before the sun dipped beneath the horizon on Saturday night, taking with it the last light of sanity, I had already collected twenty half-drunk Modelos from the rim of the boat. I poured the flat, salty remnants into the haunted lake, watching as the women went on to crack open can after can—taking approximately four sips—and then leaving them behind in search of something (was it tortilla chips? Or underwear?) in the brand-new, magical other room, where they also encounter new, shiny, unopened cans, ripe for the picking. If they were on a play-ground, it would be a juice box, and they would ditch the still-full carton to run and play; letting it wilt under its sad, chewed upon straw until inevitably getting thrown away by a stranger. I was that stranger.

Next: they love inflatables. The more colorful, the better. They need strict supervision in the water at all times. Luckily, Kate loved this; as a former lifeguard, who is also prone to reaching the point of drunkenness where she considers herself to be invincible, she took it upon herself to monitor the others. That is, until she was inebriated enough to try to swim to the nonexistent buoys, leaving the rest of the children to die in their neon-pink flamingos and sparkly inner tubes.

They fall asleep on random surfaces. They can't find their shoes. They forget what they were saying mid-sentence, and then ask you to remind them of that thing—"What was it called? What was that thing called, the one I like?"—until you remind them, which prompts them to find somewhere else to latch all of their attention. "Look over here! Watch me while I do this! Can you see me? WATCH! I love this song!"

I jot this down, noticing—quite objectively—one of the women bears a striking resemblance to a four-year-old I used to nanny, right down to the zealous fascination she gives to the microwave instructions on a Hot Pocket. Closing my notebook, I look to my left, where Annie is once again slumped into the pleather couch. Reaching between the seat cushions, she pulls out a handful of baby carrots covered in Ranch dressing.

"Huh," she mutters, placing them on her plate.

Later, I remove a tiny, sweaty pizza from the oven, and have to use a wooden spoon to bat Tiffany away from the counter long enough to slice through the blackened crust. "For the last time, Tiffany, you don't get any pizza unless you use your *nice* words," I scold her, panting.

"Bitch, just give me that pizza."

The rest happens in snapshots. There is the image of Kate dumping a handful of Now-and-Laters into her captain's hat, tossing them into the open mouths of her adoring friends as Rihanna pounds out of the Bluetooth speakers; tinny sound reverberating off the hard, desert rocks engulfing us. There is Tiffany, left breast pouring happily out of her bikini, chain-smoking American Spirits with her legs propped up on the rim of the Jacuzzi; eyes slunk down with drink, voice husking out the vivid details of her own wedding night.

There is me, scrambling up the sandy shore toward a pocket of cacti, watching the sun nestle beneath the horizon and waving to my new friend—which one is it? Is she really my friend? Is this what friends do?—as I bring my knees up to my chest, chilly and still too afraid to be sure. There is Rilo, pulling at the frayed edge of the captain's t-shirt, pursing her lips an inch from his face; because it is late, she is single, and there are no other males on this boat. Finally there is Amber, still doing her spider-monkey scramble, searching for a deck of "get-to-know-you" cards they brought to answer about Kate. Who is currently downstairs, stomping each individual syllable of "Hot in Herre" into the buckling yacht floor.

"Cassie is gonna kill me," Amber slurs, tipping back a row of red Solo cups in search of the cards. "I was supposed to bring the cards, that was the one thing I was supposed to—and if I lose them—oh *shit*," she exclaims, lifting her palm out of a pool of chunky salsa.

"We were supposed to ask the questions next," she chokes. "It was next on the agenda."

And it was. No bachelorette party would be complete without the point in the evening where a bunch of women who have known each other since college, some of them since birth, gather in a small room and drunkenly try to answer what the bride's favorite color, movie, and cocktail are. Like the cruel initiation they subjected her fiancé to, it is the unspoken test of whether a group of friends—once synced up in everything from musical taste to menstrual cycle—can possibly withstand the test of time, career, and life-altering tragedy; some spoken, some not. There's just this electric current running through them, believing that somehow—if Amber can just find the fucking trivia cards—the one weekend of debauchery will be enough to bind them again. That it may pour honey on the hearts of those who have not yet gotten what it is they think they want; and also, perhaps, the ones who have gotten it, but still don't feel whole.

Maybe there is also the comfort that comes in elevating, if only for a moment, the dreams of one of the bunch; in letting your own ego leave long enough to say *"hey, you did it; you made it; good job."* To let "I love you" flow out in tequila, and to believe in someone so much you want others to know *you* know their favorite ice-cream flavor—and you'd even pay $500 to get sick on a houseboat for them. Because not all friendships stand the test of time, nor babies, nor boundaries. But if the date of reckoning can be pushed off even one weekend longer—"Because you guys, listen to me! Thirty-five is the new twenty-five! HAVASU IS THE NEW CABO!"— then maybe it is worth it after all.

I put my pen down, pick up my personalized tumbler, and surrender. Tomorrow will bring new light; and with it, a pile of damp bathing suit bottoms, some of them still attached to people. The captain will wake up sprawled on one of the upstairs air mattresses, knowing intuitively his tiny penis has been inside of someone's mouth. There will be women in over-sized heart sunglasses, cramming their clothes into duffel bags and half-heartedly dumping old bits of sandwich into plastic trash bags. There will be talk of security deposits, stains on the carpet, and who drank the last iced coffee. There will be a riveting, serpentine drive back to the city ("THANK YOU SO MUCH, DANIELLE! OUR DESIGNATED DRIVER! WE LOVE YOU, DANIELLE!), wherein at least four people grow nauseous and need to get out. There will be panting in the desert, heads between knees, and the unparalleled Mecca of In-N-Out Burger. There will be hugs, numbers exchanged, photos air-dropped, and talk of work tomorrow. There will be more beer. But there is always more beer.

Before any of that can happen, though, I am still on the boat; Amber is still searching for the cards, and I am only just unearthing the part of myself that can float atop chaos. I wade through the parts that feel tender to touch and discover they smile—glinting—beneath my old judgments. I discover, too, Cassie says she will indeed kill Amber if she doesn't find the cards. "But after this song," she says, placing down her glittery Sharpie and admiring the mustache she's just drawn onto her sister's neck. "Kate always gets *super* slutty to this song."

I hope she finds them. I hope we all do—someday.

But in the meantime, do you want to take a shot?

To My Twenty–Two
–Year–Old Self

Before you freak out and burn all your bridges; before you throw your phone in the ocean and pierce your nose in the name of Satan and fuck that guy with a pet snake who doesn't chew his food; before you throw away every item of clothing you own and then max out your only credit card on nail polish and oven fries; and before you decide that now is the time to tell your mother every single thing she has ever done that has bothered you, and then quit your job and go back to snake guy's house, please ask yourself the following question:

Do I really desire the end of society,
or am I just dehydrated?

Me, In-Between

For a brief time at the beginning of my twenty-third winter, I was having sex. Reliably. What began as a one-night stand turned into a series of calls, then into walks around the park so we could occupy our feet in the hours before night-time; and eventually, into weekends where neither one of us felt the need to check in with Life As We Left It. For days at a time, we played house in that glorious interim: I lost my phone, and he forgot to shower.[3] I still waited until he started snoring to reach into my bedside table, groping around for earplugs; weirdly embarrassed about what I'd need in order to get a good night's sleep, but in the end, usually slipping into a tepid doze without much of a care. It would be months before I had a good night's sleep, and I knew it. I was far too busy having sex.

And so it went: in the days leading up to our sleep-ish nights, I made love to the prospect of text messages. At lunch, listening but not listening to a friend relay the arc of her recent romance, I placed my phone on the table. On vibrate, atop the menu, where I knew I'd still be able to feel it. Salad dressing on the side.

---

3. This is something that feels very cute/sexy in the phase of a relationship when you still want to take a bath in the other person's stink. It is decidedly less cute when you have been dating for, say, four years. (You know who you are.)

"I don't know," my friend told me, using a spoon to scoop up the last of her pasta. "I'm not worried. It's not like he's in any danger of falling in love with me."

Right, I thought. The danger. But what danger, exactly, was the softness of someone's fingers against her cheek? A waiter walked by with a tray of dishes, and I thought I heard my phone. In my time away from it, had love become more costly than lack?

Then, out of nowhere—before either one of us had a chance to prepare for landing— it happened: The Day. In the car with my sometimes-boyfriend, the person whose socks had gotten mixed up with mine, I felt his eyes land on my cheekbone. With both windows down, the air gusted through in a perfect, three o'clock way: behind the mountains, the only sky we could see was a blue one and the only music worth listening to was ours. I turned to meet his expression and saw for the first time the way our twenty toes had curled over the lip; saw, for the first time, the edge of the void we both stood at. At that moment, I knew the gray area was gone. For more than the sake of doing laundry, giving definition to the relationship had become as essential as breathing. We had to know which way to breathe.

Now, three days had passed since The Day. Silence lapped at the sides of my consciousness like the ocean against a steel boat. I wondered how he couldn't hear it.

Most excruciating, of course, was the fact that I did temp work as a receptionist in a law firm.[4] Sitting at my desk, drinking cup after cup of filmy coffee until the lights shook in their sockets, I questioned how anyone stays sane in the in-between. That's what I was, after all: a proxy. Someone to occupy space

---

4. This is a thing young people do when they have recently moved back to their hometown and don't want to commit to having a real™ job, and don't really know what they want to do, and would probably enjoy writing emo poetry in a coffee shop all day, but also need to make money, and most of all, need an excuse to purchase very tight "business" pants from H&M. And shoes that don't have holes.

during the time before dusk, to smile at the lawyers as they head out the door toward their vodka and tonics, to answer the phone on the off-chance it rings. Shuffling papers around in an effort to look productive, still espresso-ed beyond recognition, I scrawled a note to myself on the back of a Post-it:

YOU ARE NOT HAPPY

YOU ARE JUST CAFFEINATED

And as the last assistant walked out the door, keys jangling in her hand—electrified, giddy for the workday to be over, for real life to begin—I looked down at my phone. Two missed calls.

—

As a general rule, it takes equal parts energy to remove oneself from a relationship as it does to wiggle into it. I kept this in mind as I stood in the parking lot; phone pressed against my ear, listening to my sometime-boyfriend do the dance of indecision.

"I'm just not emotionally available," he told me. "And it's not fair to you. I'm still in love with someone else." The phone made a tinny sound, and I flipped back to The Day; the way sunlight had streamed in the window, demanding we pick a side. I'd picked mine, it's true. He cleared his throat. "But I still want to be friends! Nothing has to change."

And indeed, nothing changed; not that evening, as I white-knuckled home with my hands on the wheel, sobbing so hard my glasses fogged up. Not the next evening, when my friend held my hand—listening but not listening, her phone at the edge of the couch—and I wondered if I'd ever be somebody's now, instead of somebody's placeholder. Not even down the road, when my used-to-be-sometime-boyfriend was back with his girlfriend, but still had me over to watch a movie. And we sat there, and he stroked my face with the tip of his thumb. I realized this was a man for whom Action and Intention occupied different continents: as long as he stayed in the latter, he was safe on the beach of monogamy. He didn't intend to start kissing me. But he did, and I remembered he hadn't wanted to be my boyfriend, and I remembered the part of "having your cake and eating it too," and I wondered if I was the cake, and then—before I even had a chance to realize what was happening—I was getting up. I knew I wanted something better. And just like that, I was free. Whether Action or Intention, someone had their hand up my shirt, and I sneered at them both. And riding the wave of clarity—a budding feeling I would fade in and out of over my twenties—I realized. It was time to go home.

(I've never understood it when someone asks, "What do you expect? I'm only human."

It is so much, this human thing.)

⌒

There is something cruelly beautiful about the five a.m. hour. In that space before the sun rises, neither here nor there, it is easy to mistake its gelatinous quality for something unreal: like a sleep eater on Ambien, I used to spend early morning drives from my quasi-boyfriend's house stuffing fistfuls of trail mix into my mouth. *If it happens while half-conscious, it doesn't quite count.* It's true transitional phases exist, and transitional people—lost as they get in the folds of memory—well, they exist too. There is a hopeless romance hardwired in me; however, the mindset that sees two dead rats in the road and thinks, "Well, at least they had each other," is the same one that sees an abandoned freeway, sun cresting over the horizon, and feels nothing but groundedness. Reverence for the ordinary, for the five o'clock hour, for utter confusion, for being between. For the day that came, and the day just beginning — for the person who will one day dial my number, the one who knows all the words to the songs I've forgotten I love — and for being a temporary receptionist: paid fourteen dollars an hour to do what I was already doing for free. Staring at a phone, waiting for it to ring.

No Really

*N*o really, tell me one more time
Just what kind of person I am.

One whose dress snags the tide
And a full-moon stare
For as long as it takes you to leave.

In my mind, I can still hear you leave.

No really, tell me, while you're here,
Just what kind of lover I am.

One whose kisses are contracts
Between your non-parties,
Between asterisks, where
Just between you and me,
There's no boundary,
No line to cross.

The edge only comes when things meet.

No really, tell me one more time,
Just what kind of woman I am.

One who smears against walls made of paper tomorrows
Out tumbling somewhere in space.

Not to mention the person who sits on the bed,
Knees tucked up like patience,
Who pulls briny poems from your ear with her tongue,
And then slips from the scene like a fog.

No really, tell me. I'm dying to know.

Tell me what kind of body I am.

One who thrashes too eagerly, drunk and in love,
With the feeling of wet against skin,
Who can light, but refuses to hold any breath.

For a water that's only waist deep.

Too open is only too open to crack
Through layers too lazy to form.
Seems like everything makes its way over to bad.
You crawled inside mine to stay warm.

Oh wise one, enlighten me,
One more time.

Tell me how my existence feeds yours.

And then leeches from it, howling you into vent,
All without seeing me,
All without my consent.

Oh darling, open me. One more time.
Wind me up in the palm of your hand.

If you hadn't informed me, how could I know
How disgustingly present I am?

No really. Watch me. Taking in stride
The work that I did without you.
And see me. Finally, coming alive.

Your silence is long overdue.

The Seven Stages of Alone

Like most roads to hell, it is paved with vision boards. Watered with four-dollar wine and the metaphorical blood of the men who have "wronged you." There is at least one volume of sad poetry and one cheap spiral notebook which you will label your "INTENTION JOURNAL" and stare at each night before going to bed, with every intention of cataloging your intentions, but will, instead, watch four hours of *Lifetime* original movies. Which, like most roads to hell, are paved with vision boards.

STAGE ONE: SHOCK

It's a Nicholas Sparks world, and we're all just buying tampons in it and, at some point, you probably meant to be here. You probably caught a movie (or twelve) that taught you that to live the life of your dreams, you must have one of two things:

1. an easily accessible window, should John Cusack arrive with a boombox, or
2. a self-induced period of solitude in your twenties, preferably in a rent-controlled apartment, preferably one with exposed brick.

And, at some point, the sea of boyfriends parts, left in their place, an echoey chorus of "I'm just not *ready*" and the expanse of that which you always thought you thought you wanted. Alone. A space, while sanctioned by sitcoms, remaining exhaustingly absent from the cultural consensus on womanhood. Everyone tells you to spend time alone. No one seems to understand, nor believe, you are. That the beast of your life leading up to this point, every dream you had for the people you'd loved, has sunk its teeth into your apartment. Noticeably absent of exposed brick. Likely missing several essential qualities, like street parking and toilet paper.

You tell yourself being alone is the nature of life. But you had a plan for yours, and it did not involve Tinder nor minimum wage.

You tell yourself you chose this; you use words like *energy* and say you're keeping yours safe. You recall all of your romantic failures in alphabetical order and finally understand Tom Waits' songs. A rawness begins to creep from your skin, and you label it Shock. You commit to its tiny bursts of mania; you move your bed to the opposite corner, and in those precious moments when you've first woken up, there's the Shock of forgetting whose house you are in. In that moment you are clear, crystal clear, no one stands between you and the weight of what you believe could have happened. You feel more aware than you want to.

That's probably around the time you enter denial. The voice in your head, tired of listing your pain, downs a vat of espresso and says things like, "This is GREAT! I love (walking on the beach, having meaningful conversations, inventing problems) being by myself! In fact, I'd choose this. I can't believe I ever thought that I needed to go to restaurants with other people. There are so many people here on dates. That must really suck for them."

It says, "If I wanted to, I could totally be out with friends. Sure, I'm home eating Cheerios out of a water tumbler. But

I'm just really into spending time with myself." You sign up for things like Intro to Weaving and spend $60 on a gym membership which you exclusively use for the sauna.

"I'm sorry, I can't. I'm on my way to the gym."

You lose half a pound from sweating so much and think you're probably glowing, just like pregnant women do. You wonder if maybe you're pregnant but realize you need to have sex to be that . . . so you take up Pilates. You spend all your money on face wash and cheese.

You feel more aware than you want to.

STAGE TWO: PAIN AND GUILT

Nowhere in the course of common etiquette are we taught how to accompany other people on their dates. There's no class on third wheeling. When cozying up to watch a movie, how close is too close? When they begin kissing for longer than three seconds, do you look away? All your friends are coupled up—was it always this way? There's a secret they all have, a magical code, and the longer you spend outside of its circle, the more foreign its boundaries feel. Your friends invite you to watch the sunset, and the three of you stand in a row; you sense the ease in which they fold into one another.

"It's perfect," one whispers, the rest of their sentence escaping the reach of your ear. Your pedestrian ear. Your ringing, pedestrian ear.

You think of your nights spent alone, so many opportunities to write your manifesto, and calculate the percentage that has instead been spent researching the family histories of minor celebrities.

You calculate the number of social media platforms on which to experience the pain of rejection and divide that number by one. Immoveable, unyielding, one. Exponential on birthdays, holidays, and the soft hours of the morning—the time you've forgotten you're sleeping alone.

Left with nothing but time to consider your faults, you come to the reasonable conclusion every breakup has been completely your fault. You write a ~~50 page novella~~ super casual email to your ex displaying the contents of your deepest child-hood shame, certain it is the root of your howling discomfort. In a fit of caffeine, you hit send. In the conspiracy show that is life you're the star, and you're dying alone. You're all *slowly dying alone.*

You finish this thought with a flourish of pen and close your INTENTION JOURNAL—its contents now entirely populated with your hurt. Your hurt. The thing, at least, you can grip. Your phone buzzes, and you lunge expectantly. A voice says, "I actually have plans with my [girlfriend, husband, college roommate, OkCupid date] tonight, but you're welcome to join! We're thinking Chinese food."

Your wallet is within reach. There's no price you'd not pay to lift over the rim of this pain.

STAGE THREE: ANGER AND BARGAINING

"No, YOU listen, evil demon who lives in my mind: I'm fine. I'm totally, fucking, fine. You think you're lonely? Great. I'll show you lonely. I'll take your lonely and kick its sorry little ass, and then slather it with the burned pages of all the books that I swore I never had time to read, only now I have the time, and I realize I don't fucking *want* to read another *fucking* story about how great that new-agey chick's life became when she set off to travel the world alone. Because you know what she had? *Money.* And you know what else she had? A harem of European men telling her how brave and special she was for traveling *alone,* which we all know is bullshit, because I've traveled alone before, and all I got was a fucking *stomach parasite.* Which, in case you were wondering, is not a metaphor. But speaking of metaphors, FUCK everyone."

STAGE FOUR: DEPRESSION, REFLECTION, AND LONELINESS

It occurs to you, while trying to button the back of your skirt, you could walk into the world with a stain on your butt and not know until a stranger points it out. Which they do. Twice. For some reason, it's this thought that pins you to the parking lot, unable to pick up your keys. You manage to walk into the grocery store, but nothing looks good. You believe this is the right time to casually explore herbal wellness and leave the aisle forty minutes later convinced you need Echinacea and an entirely new life. You don't know if you drink the right water. The cashier asks you a question, and the words on your lips are like cotton. It feels like you need to say something, but you're not sure which answer is yours.

On your way out, you pass a porch of happy-hour margarita drinkers and realize you are staring . . . much in the same way a teenage boy stares at a bag of Doritos. Starving. You've had a rash on your arm for days and, after several hours of Googling, are no longer convinced you have cholera; however, you also have memorized most major cities in Canada, and that felt like a good use of time.

You dig into the pool of feeling at the pit of your stomach, hoping for water. You stare at your phone and sometimes it rings and sometimes you say yes to a party and often show up in a dress. Other times, you politely decline. "Thank you, but I've forgotten how to interact with other humans. Plus, I have these new pore strips which I'm dying to use."

You watch all six seasons of *Gossip Girl* and only feel mildly sorry. You consider the number of single women who have choked on a walnut and died alone and think your mother would call you before you had a chance to properly decompose . . . and position your phone in the only space where you know it gets service. Your grandmother's number appears, and your voice cracks as you answer, loaded with suddenly needing to make something heard.

"My voice cracks when I try to sing," she says. "My vocal chords just don't get the exercise they used to."

She's alone for the first time in sixty-five years, and you wish you had talked to your grandpa more. Wish you had asked him, *Grandpa, do you play that music so loud so that you don't have to hear your own mind?* You picture him, arms crossed at his chest, and wish you had shown him your heart. Wish you could come home with someone worth sixty-five years. You wish that someone was you.

"I talk to myself," you tell your grandma. All the time.

"So do I," she says. "But mainly to yell at the TV."

You sit late at night in a tub full of salt and quickly learn which full-length Disney movies are available for free on the Internet. You cry at their Oscar-winning soundtracks. You were counting on that. Counting on fingers, on the backs of hands that you never looked at so closely before, hands that look like your mother's—the number of days you've spent with the feeling nothing will change. You remember the times you sat on the playground, middle school rising like steam on a lake, and tucked your head into your knees to avoid looking up. You knew what was ending. You knew what was starting as well.

You know even now, in that tender space between your knees, how loneliness likes to be held.

STAGE FIVE: THE UPWARD TURN

You feel back for the buttons on your skirt. You befriend them. You fumble for your keys in the parking lot. You befriend them. You grab two gallons of generic water. You befriend them. The grocery clerks ask would you like a receipt? You befriend them.

You pass by strangers, drunk in the sun. You befriend them. You look at the bumps on your arm. You befriend them. You realize everyone leaves. You befriend them. You sit with your head at your knees. You befriend them. You stare at the tops of your hands. You befriend them. You look at your life up to now. You long for the one coming soon. You cry for the years you have left. You befriend them.

STAGE SIX: RECONSTRUCTION AND WORKING THROUGH

You're alone. You come home at night and sit on the bed and there you are, alone. It's simple, so beautifully simple, so opposite of every relationship you've ever waited for *yes* to bleed out of. You pinch to find blood in your cheeks. You look at yourself in the mirror, and it's enough to make you want to kiss every bone of your spine. It's enough to understand Tom Waits. It's enough.

You realize you don't actually like *Gossip Girl*. You never did. You decide the internet is a place for free yoga videos and home remedies for hair loss and vow to use it for good. You laugh out loud in an empty room. You draw pictures of places with tall grasses and wind and bookmark an award-winning documentary on cyber-bullying. You vow to become an ally. Your life is the thing that's for good, and you plant flowers at each place your inner sidewalk cracks.

You realize, at some point during this time alone, you've stopped chasing people who don't want to be found. You realize the one you'd been after all along, and you tuck her into bed. You feed her raspberries. She sleeps on her back now, eyes pointed upward. She likes waking early. She feels it all, and it's not too much.

STAGE SEVEN: ACCEPTANCE AND HOPE

When you were little, your mom used to tell you stories of fairies in faraway lands. "Once upon a time," she'd say, "Thumbelina would wait by the window 'til the prince flew up on his magical bumblebee—"

"Magical BUMBLEBEE?"

". . . Yes, his, um, magical bumblebee. So the prince would arrive on his magical bumbl—"

"But where did he get that, though? Do you have—do you know where he—like, was the BEE magical, or did he put magic ON the—"

"It was already magical. The bee was already magical. The prince arrived with his magical bee, and Thumbelina climbed out the window, and they fell in love and rode away into the night . . . and they lived happily ever after."

It has taken you most of your life until now to realize you might be the bee. To remember how it felt to be pressed against your mother's shoulder as she spoke, heart like a drum, soft body telling you—as long as she is—you are never alone.

It has taken you most of your life to make peace with the garden inside you—to tend it, like you would anything that you love, with water. With silence. With air. And one night, as you are falling asleep, you feel something new breathe into your veins: like a tale from a faraway land. Foreign. Yet utterly yours.

You revise.

Once upon a time, a girl sat with her hands on top of the wheel, staring out the window of her car. She has nowhere to be, not quite yet. She's no longer digging for Yes. She believes in the love that comes rushing from mountain tops and turns up the radio. Loud. She pulls from the curb and starts thinking maybe she got here right on time. Nothing more. Nothing needed. Not yet.

She is humming with notes.

She is earning her keep.

And she lives happily into her after.

PART II:

New

Boys Don't Cry

FIG. 1: Life, also known as a series of mishaps where the person you have THAT feeling for knows exactly what you're talking about because they have it for someone else.

I listen to music when I drive. It's all I do, really: the driving is secondary, the thing my hands accomplish while the rest squirms inside whatever song happens to be playing. My car radio has lost its digital display, and I have no idea if I'm gambling for soft rock or NPR. Then Celine Dion comes on, and I know. Then another song plays, and I wonder at what point a person should become concerned that she can differentiate which version of "Everybody Dance Now" is performed by C&C Music Factory. Like, a normal person wouldn't know that. They just wouldn't.

As a child, I remember understanding what it meant to be a grown-up. It was simple: being grown-up meant watching *Glitter* in solitude. To this day, I've never seen the film, and yet I vividly remember listening to a twenty-something in my childhood ballet company discuss her plans to go home and order takeout, sewing her Nutcracker costume while Mariah Carey lit up the screen with her bare belly. I remember this, the distinct wave of lust for what it meant to eat Thai food by oneself, bits of costume scattered across cheap carpeting, while the oily noodles got trapped in my grown-up teeth and left a film of garlic on my grown-up tongue.

Thoughts like this enter my brain now and again, disguised as poetry. A broken hymn of paragraph alignment. Cereal dust at the bottom of the box. For example:

What do you do, exactly,
when you find someone else's child to be disgusting?
What do you do in that moment
when everyone fawns over this kid—
usually six or seven years old—
and you have to excuse yourself to go to the bathroom,
where the perfect
asymmetry of that horrifying child's mouth
can't possibly follow you?

My brain has lost its digital display, and some people give me the heebie-jeebies for no reason. Others, whether they like it or not, swim into my bloodstream before I've had a chance to check their passport at the door. One second I am a normal person with a pulse and pockets in my jeans, and the next every ounce of me is full. There's no backtracking. There's no crying in baseball.

There's only this: the possibility of you and the way your posture changed when I walked over. The way you brought me into your body without knowing what it meant, what it could possibly mean to someone like me, destiny dotting the notches of my spine like quarter notes. I want to tell you that you have Peter Pan eyes, but you won't even know it's me.

Cue music.

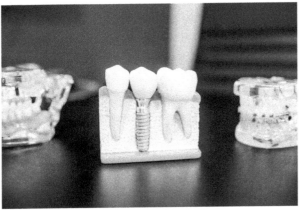

Fig. 2: It has been six months since your last check up!

We hold emotion in our teeth. Love and loss run a map along the molar line, peaking and plowing with the soft tissue encircling each mound of our past. I thought of this as I lay back, trying not to suck my dentist's finger while he charted the progress of my receding gums to Kathy, the hygienist, like coordinates on a plane.

"Number 28, 2. Number 27, 4." She scribbled the answers on a legal pad, and though I couldn't see her, I knew she wouldn't be smiling. She never does. She may be the only dental hygienist in the world not to use the time when she's prying my mouth open, teeth coated in saccharine grit, as an opportunity to make conversation.

"So how's school?"

"Etth haaawd but etth gooooth."

"Oh GOOD! So what are you studying? How is your mom? How's the weather outside? What do you want to be when you grow up? How many licks does it take to get to the center of a Tootsie Roll Pop? What are the first twenty-five digits of pi? What's the secret of everlasting life?"

And because she doesn't, I want her to. Because she buzzes my mouth clean without a word, nothing but watery mascara and respectful silence, I resent her. The universal exacerbation at chatty hygienists, the faux frustration of "Oh, Kathy with her incessant questioning. . . . Can't she see I have my mouth full?" . . . I want in on it. Because she doesn't, I want her to. I want her to care.

The dentist took his hand out of my mouth and discussed the tiny, perfect line of red running along the bottom left side.

"Want to see?" He held up the mirror, and I felt the slickness of each tooth, sweeping up the blood with my tongue.

Exposed nerve, sensitive as a sneeze. I wonder what point in the relationship exactly—my relationship to love, that thing that lodged itself in the emotional catastrophe of my bottom teeth—was powerful enough to wear away the gum tissue, steady but soft, like baking soda at the bottom of a tub. February 2010, perhaps?

"The good news is it's not getting any worse. So whatever you're doing, keep it up."

I made a mental note to continue eating chocolate chips out of the bag, watching Netflix from underneath about six comforters while autumn makes its steady approach into the crevices of my hut. I left the dentist that day with a packet of toothpaste and two soft-bristle brushes, taking comfort in the fact—no matter where I am, no matter what my gums are doing—in six months' time, someone will think of me enough to send a self-addressed photo of a squirrel flossing its teeth. Someone somewhere will take note of the fact that my mouth is not clean.

AUSTIN, TX
POPULATION: 842,592

FIG. 3: In which Doris Gets Her Oats

It is true most accidents happen within a few miles of home, and the likelihood of a plane crash is always heightened during takeoff and landing. It is also true that somewhere on the planet, a person exists whose only job is to determine these statistics: to measure them with a spoon and inflate till they're meaningful. Nevertheless, I spend each and every second a plane begins its initial ascent with my hands folded tightly in my lap, praying and praying and praying. My mom cries, and I pray. Then we both drink soda, which we almost never do.

Just as food tastes better—saltier, somehow—ordinary quandaries take on new meaning from the perspective of an airtight metal box hurtling miles above the ground. For example: Why do planes bother to have a no-smoking light? It's not as though they're ever going to turn it off, like suddenly, "*Ding!* All this time we've warned you not to tamper with the smoke detector in the lavatory, we've just been testing your attention. Congratulations! You've solved the puzzle, and as a reward, we're going to turn off the no-smoking light. The entire aircraft is now a floating tobacco zone. Smoke up, people."

I pondered in silence, reading the safety instruction card and grossing out over how many people had touched it before me. I guessed how many times I could walk to the bathroom out of sheer boredom before 17A would request a seat change, assuming some sort of horrific digestive disorder on my part that could cause my bowels to explode at any moment. I ate my Clif bar deliberately, mysteriously, getting up every half hour . . . but she didn't seem to notice.

As we sped closer to Austin, I slept with my head crunched into the tray table. With every moment passing in the flight, I let my brain float toward him: like a reel, I pictured the beginning of each scene, dropping it before it had a chance to spoil in logistics. In specificity. I pictured him without a voice attached, like we were players in a movie montage neither one of us made. Fog lay heavy on a cold beach. I remembered the look he gave with his head tilted down, eyes smiling, upper lip turned in at the seams, then stopped because I realized I was actually remembering a *Lifetime* movie. The scene, that is. Not the smile.

Do you think we manifest things on the ground the way we do in the air, miles above the feeling of feet on pavement?

His smile continued to visit me that weekend, appearing in corners and cobwebs and shoes. Everything became a cog in the dream I'd created for myself; that machine of instant karma rendering every action meaningful. Suddenly, it's all an opportunity: no dishwasher emptied, no door held open without the blind hope it will earn enough street cred for a desire to come true.

On Friday night, standing in the bathroom line behind two girls—each one tugging on the hem of her microscopic skirt, fingers laden in thick, plastic turquoise—a third voice came from inside a stall. "Does anyone have any *gum*? It's an emergency." Tug, tug, pull, pull. Silence. It was then I saw my opportunity. And as I handed my last piece of Trident underneath the door, I decided that was it: the deed that would put me over the karmic brink and into the land of granted wishes. "Ohmigod, THANK YOU." Tug, tug, pull, pull. I pictured my wish and tucked myself into an open stall. *You're welcome.*

When I arrived at White Horse the next night, I saw him from across the porch. *Of course. It's you.* And as I made my way over to his side of the world, all cool anticipation and unspoken promises, I locked into cruise control: I'd done what I could do. The rest was him, all him, and the type of honkytonk music that takes a bite out of the moon.

⌐

AUSTIN, TX
POPULATION: 2

Barreling down the freeway, the massive weight of the tour van shimmying from side to side as we changed lanes, I flicked on the radio. A jazz singer plucked out the first few chords of a song by The Cure, and I slunk down in my seat. *I hate covers,* I told him, remembering 311's rendition of "Lovesong" and its significance to my first boyfriend. The one who had another girlfriend but still took me to the Homecoming Dance. Bottom left molar, number 25.

"Try liking them." He chuckled and turned up the volume.

Something about loving you,
Something about staying,
But you're already gone.

He rounded the corner and brought the van into park, humming to stillness at the curb outside my house. "I used to play on this street as a kid," he said, looking out the window. "That weighs heavily on me."

I know it does.

Something about limits,
And then someone pushes too far.

"What do you want?" he asked, breath halting as my hand ran slowly, surely, along the seam of his shirt, feeling the contour of each pearl button like the surface of a slick tooth. *I'm not sure, I answered. But what I know is I won't run away, this time, into the woods behind your van. What I want is to stay.*

Something about getting you to come back,
By my side,
But someone just laughs.

"Come here."

Their tears are invisible.

At one point, our hair got tangled together, and I'm sure I laughed. "I'm not able to give myself lovingly to anyone right now," he whispered, the energy between us still tangible as clay. "I'm only just learning to be there for myself." *Me too,* I told him but, just like that, I got it.

I knew how it felt to bring something into being, to fall ferociously toward a human—if only for a night—because they are a walking, breathing totem of all the things that *you* can be. To pour into one another like water down a throat. I realized what Sheila Heti meant when she said some of us are destined to be exposed, to be sliced open like a tomato for all our insides to be seen, simply because we must; we have to show ourselves, two halves rocking toward one another from the stickiness of their plate, because others will learn. They will learn from our stickiness and sweetness and light and our willingness—sometimes—to curl into someone completely, not knowing what it is going to be, for the sheer purpose of uncovering a piece of our own heart.

> *Something about boys,*
> *They don't cry,*
> *They don't cry,*
> *They don't cry.*

There are soulmates, you know, all over this land. Your soulmate is not the one you share your secrets with. Your soulmate is the one who misses you too.

FIG. 4: "I am a free witch I have nooo guuilt"

UNIVERSE: So, Jenna, why is it so important for you to get a "real" job?

JENNA: Because, Universe, when I'm feeling emotional, I get drunk and buy things on Etsy.

The following week, I made my way out to babysit in Goleta; the next stop in my one-woman show, *The incredible disappearing autonomy! Come one, come all; watch how the lovesick puppy attempts to function like a human being!* Though I pretended otherwise, an emotional wave had crashed. My heart lay heavy in my chest, like a moon slung low in the sky.

Bearing no sensitivity for such things, Ian—the eight-year-old—ushered me into his room and shut off the lights. "Watch," he instructed, fiddling with something behind his fish tank. His room, a perfect microcosm of elementary school, was splattered with glow-in-the-dark stars; and for a moment, I stopped disappearing. "Look!" he said, holding up the type of light sold to the children of scientists and doctors. "It's plasma! *Plasma*, I tell you."

Looking around the room of lights, I thought I spotted Saturn. Would it be possible for me to give, just this once, without expecting anything in return? Where is the power in that? Then again, where *isn't* the power in that?

Later that evening, Ian poring over his math homework, I sat with *Sibley Bird Guide* in my lap. As I made my way past starlings and scrub jays, egrets and raptors, I couldn't help but notice the males always have the best costume. They're far more vibrant, more colorful. Compensating for personality, perhaps? Or is it just that some creatures have to be shockingly beautiful so the rest of us can hurtle toward them, tail feathers to the wind, hoping to absorb a bit of their magic? I continued turning the pages, wondering which of these birds—if any—would be me. I ran my finger over certain distinguishing qualities: *red-faced, solitary.* I remembered that night in Austin, tracing my fingers along his sweat-sticky belly, watching the traffic light change outside the van window. I had asked him what his soul's animal was.

"I can't tell you," he said. *Why not?*

"I just can't."

Because, dear one, to define something is to resurrect its opposite. Some things must remain unspoken in order to retain their power. Some things, it seems, are better left unsaid.

Some things. Not all things. Not this thing. Not you.

Ian's head snapped up, breaking my stupor. "Hey, do you want to make tops out of Legos and then battle them to see whose spins the longest?" Nope. Not in the slightest bit, not even a little tiny bit. No. *Okay,* I answered. *Of course.*

So we did.

The day I left Austin, standing in the airport, a wave of clarity had run through my body—so electric, so pure—that I nearly mistook it for truth.

Standing in front of the floor-to-ceiling windows, sleeplessness inflating my muscles like air, I knew only that I was powerful: alive and potently aware of my own strength. This is what it means to be human, after all. To listen to loud music as you come up the driveway, unafraid of what others will think; to let them move you, to move them, to heal and fight and fuck each other until there's nothing left but love. Love, and the gift of colliding—not long enough to leave a dent, perhaps, but long enough to leave a note.

Standing there, I understood. Tomorrow would be devastating, right on schedule; the week that followed, full of losses and tiny victories. Farmer's market flowers, making tops from Legos. That sort of thing. But today, watching planes pull butt-first onto the tarmac—ready to take flight—I still got to feel what it meant to be free. To let an experience be healing by virtue of the fact it rips you wide open: to rip wide open and feel beautiful too. In spite of the fact I may always love you here, in this place between lines, in my imperfect way. In spite of the fact I still have your smell in my hair. In spite of it all.

Drive

I used to define myself by my sex drive.
    As in, having a high one, and then taking it
on cross country trips.
Hopping out at a stoplight and switching seats
So that they always knew I was fun.

No one ever wants to define themselves by their low drive.
I'd listen to new mothers complain, myself not one
Yet.
And I'd hear them say not my boobs, he always wants to
touch my boobs,
And I want to throw him off a cliff,
And I'd think: not me.
When my time comes, I'll have gas in the tank,
And if not, I will suck it up.

Just like I always have.
Like the men had always told me. To suck
It up in one way or another
Because that is what we do in order to keep one another
Alive.

And they'd disappear behind closed doors, or missed calls,
And I'd think
I'll show you—I'll drive us both out of here
On a chicken wing prayer for that day to never come
When I might have to face myself.

Because the truth is, I am only a human woman.
Too smart not to realize that the patriarchy is trying to sell me
Just one more thing, to maybe be good enough.
But
Too human not to buy it anyway
And smear it into the lines on my face
That I don't remember getting
Probably last Friday in line at the DMV.

And maybe the truth is I just want to be kissed
The way my gut fireworks when I watch it in the movies,
That first kind of kiss
And I want it even though I wouldn't trade what I have
Just to drive off the cliff one more time.

I am a human woman also but not only
Don't call me by your name
See me
for my change.

Scott and I Meditate

*Y*ou know the type.

They've probably stood next to you in the aisle of Whole Foods. While both of you studied gluten-free crackers, they've offered a piece of unsolicited advice about the ratio of protein to sodium levels. They told you they tried a similar cracker while on retreat in Tulum, and it changed their life. They could feel in their gut-chakra they had been holding some unresolved anger toward their mother, and eating these crackers really helped them eliminate their emotional traumas. (Well, it was that and the organic coffee enemas.) They will hold their hand out, and upon seeing you go for the somewhat obvious suggestion of a handshake, will pull you instead for a smothering hug; letting out a muffled "I'm a HUG person" midway through a bone-crushing embrace, before releasing you into a cloud of palo santo oil (rubbed into their beard, obvs) and offering to take your phone number. Like they are doing you a colossal favor, like you'd be so lucky to be the recipient of a ten-minute courtesy fuck between yoga classes, because they are just so sexy; and like you, they enjoy gluten-free crackers. Which you will end up purchasing for them, somehow? For the rest of eternity.

I'm talking about the Spiritual Fuckboi.[5] Reporting now as I am from the dirt-poor—yet emotionally sovereign—throne of my thirties, I am able to better reflect on the role this particular phenomena of maleness has played in my sense of self, my relationships, and virtually every therapy appointment I have had since the tender age of twenty-three. The Whole Foods boi is a typecast; but the truth is this trope of a troubadour has been ravaging communities (in Southern California) for Goddess knows how long and will continue unless they are stopped in their tracks. Take away their discount codes for Lululemon! Burn all the copies of *Sex at Dawn*, unless they are willing to read it in full instead of referencing a few poorly skimmed sections in order to justify their primary manifesto, that Monogamy Isn't Natural for Humans! If I had a dollar for every beautiful, braided man in mala beads who told me he had just become spiritually actualized, and from it, had realized he needed to put his penis into many people in rotation instead of choosing just one hole to focus on (I'm paraphrasing), I would not need to clip coupons for the grocery store or even write this book. I would be far too busy sitting in my swimming pool of HUNDRED DOLLAR BILLS.

I was born and spend most of my waking hours in Southern California, where this particular caricature seems to grow on trees and has only been given more power since Instagram came around and granted them a platform to post insanely hot yoga videos, or juicing tutorials, or white-boy spiritual chanting. You see, one of the primary characteristics of the Spiritual Fuckboi is he uses connection to God, spirit, art, or some watered-down version of Buddhism to justify and/or mask his undeniably fuckboi-ish behavior; think a dude who doesn't call you back for three weeks after having sex and then claims it is because he has been on a silent retreat

---

5. At the time of this writing, "fuckboi" is neither flagged nor spellchecked by Google. I can't decide if this is invigorating or traumatizing.

or "just doesn't buy into the technology conspiracy." He is probably named Tad, or Jherem, or Surdu Acorn (his chosen name). You know the type.

And as I mentioned, I certainly know the type. In fact, I have been exposed enough over my life to have gained partial immunity; at least, that's what I tell myself when I'm watching a sculpted man teach me about basket weaving and feel nothing. I am still moderately vulnerable to the Spiritual Fuckboi with a musicianship/hiking rising, a rare breed gaining its power from borrowing your car for weeks at a time and bringing home seashells that "remind them of you." But there aren't enough pages in the world to get into that dumpster fire, so I'll focus here on just a few of the originals.

It's worth noting they aren't all dangerous. Lucas, for example, was one of the innocents. Insufferable, but innocent. When I first met him, I had recently moved back to the US from a long-term stay in Bali, Indonesia. And before you go all *Eat, Pray, Love* on my ass, let me explain: Liz Gilbert had only just written that book. Instagram wasn't a thing yet, and influencers didn't exist. I fixated on Bali because it was about the farthest I could get from home; and, at the last minute, was given money to teach English at a small school after the first grantee dropped out. (Sloppy seconds aren't a thing when it's a free plane ticket to Indonesia.)

What began as seven weeks morphed into a year. I finally shed the skin of a long-term codependent relationship, fell in love with the island, found another job, and stayed.

So when I met Lucas, I was fresh. Like a little peeled egg. I walked into our local yoga studio because it smelled like the incense I'd just spent the past year inhaling and sat down next to a white man in yoga pants, which I'd just spent the last year avoiding. He also wore several strings of wooden beads and was journaling. Nay: DIARY-ING. I don't know much, but I know Lucas was definitely diary-ing. After looking up at me several times, he finally put his pen down, closed his eyes for emphasis, and cooed, *"Hello, there."*

"Um . . . hello!" I said, a little startled. I had only just remembered people speak English. I'll cut to the chase: within about two minutes of ~~monologue~~ conversation, wherein Lucas established he was a) super into yoga, b) super into people who do yoga, and c) definitely not working what one might call a "real job," he asked me if I wanted to exchange numbers. He regularly led something called Kirtan, which I had become familiar with in Bali. Basically, it's a call-and-response style singing ceremony entirely conducted in Sanskrit, is commonly practiced in Hindu cultures, and was not something I knew a white man even knew about, let alone led. I was intrigued. He texted me within twenty-four hours,[6] asking if I wanted to get to know one another better and meet at a local business specializing in selling authentic Asian furniture and handicrafts at a 3,000 percent upcharge. They happened to have a koi pond in the back, which is perfect for lounging. Sign me up!

While I knew I was not interested in Lucas romantically, it took me about five seconds of arriving at our Super Casual Koi Meetup to realize Lucas did not have the same knowledge. He also, as it turned out, had very little basic knowledge of what it takes to have a reciprocal human interaction. And I say this with empathy. But there wasn't one minute in our interaction, not ONE TEENY MINUTE, where I was asked anything about myself. I know this because I had ample time to assess what he had chosen to wear (linen pants, scarf printed with lotus blossoms, multiple bracelets printed with the faces of Hindu goddesses). I listened as he told me what he did during most of his days: went to the gym, meditated.

---

6. At this point in my dating life, I had only really become acquainted with one type of fuckboi: the dirty musician who doesn't text you back. I was brainwashed into thinking normal human texting behavior was the Holy Grail. I blame this for many subsequent years of Pavlovian, knee-jerk trust in any man who actually texts first. Note: This does not mean they are a good person. This means they have thumbs.

That's it.

I listened as he told me what he did for work; as it turns out, Lucas had made a shitload of money on Wall Street, and then spent it all to move to California and pursue what he called "intuitive financial consulting." I asked him what that meant and, to this day, I could not tell you even one thing. Mostly, he just enjoyed meditating and working out and leading Kirtan ceremonies, which he infused with his own original singer-songwriter jams. "Because I don't want to compete," he said. With what? With centuries-old sacred text and music?

I sat chewing my ginger candy and imagining he must have experienced hardship at some point in his life. I looked into his watery brown eyes, assessed the smattering of freckles running across his nose, and imagined him as an innocent child. This is one of my favorite exercises to do when someone is pissing me off, and I don't know why. But then the tea we ordered was delivered to our table, and we were given an option of green tea or something called Love tea. Lucas didn't ask what I wanted. "We'll have Love," he said. "Because I think it's best to choose love." And then I knew why.

When our *compostable* paper cups were filled with Love and Lucas had made a toast ("To us," he said, boring into my eyes with what can only be described as grotesque focus), he proceeded to launch into a forty-five-minute diatribe about why "letting go is better than holding on." No prompt.

I began picking at my cuticles and determined I must be an atrocious bitch to feel so murderous toward someone I had just met, who was only trying to lecture me on the importance of "respecting Mamma Gaia," but after thirty more minutes of listening to Lucas describe his favorite salad bars in Santa Barbara, I decided I didn't care. I thanked him for inviting me, and he put his index finger to my lips. "Don't thank me. Thank the universe."

"I just listened. Listening is SO important," he finished, adjusting his goddess beads.

We walked out to the car, and I decided I would take three showers when I got home. He asked where I typically spend my work hours, and I told him I did remote grant writing work and posted up at a local coffee shop. He shuddered.

"I can't go to that coffee shop. I'm just *really* sensitive to energy."

I casually mentioned my (nonexistent) boyfriend three times before leaving, thanked Lucas again for the invitation, and drove home in my old Toyota that, according to him, was killing the Earth. I didn't practice intuitive finance. I didn't even have a credit card. And I proceeded to launch into five more years of giving myself away at a high interest rate, giving my time to men like Lucas, only with a different kind of spell; saying yes when what I really wanted to do was run.

———

I mention Lucas as one of the innocents because I genuinely believe he is a good person, in his heart. He meant well. He just didn't understand exclusively talking about one's own spiritual and creative practice—largely appropriated from another culture and given zero acknowledgment as such—was a little, how do we say? Masturbatory. But the only reason I found him so intolerable was I had not yet experienced the joy of having someone *actually* masturbate in front of me without consent and then pass it off as being "sexually liberated."

That precious era arrived in my life not long after I met Lucas. I worked as a grant writer and dance teacher and had been introduced to a community of local artists who had started a festival that was gaining a lot of momentum. They were hosting a promotional event at my local dance studio, and I attended without question. After all, this was a group of AR-TEESTS! They had been to Burning Man! They were worldly! They were cultured! They were holding my hand! Well, one of them was. A tall, dark-eyed, dimpled man with paint underneath his fingernails stamped my hand to ensure my entrance into the event, and then didn't let go.

"Hi," he said. "I'm Ben."

And apparently that was all I needed to hear.

Over the course of the next several months, Ben and I began meeting up at odd hours—always at his initiation and never at his house. I'm embarrassed to say I didn't find anything wrong with this, at least not at first. I like to blame the fact I had so recently been in a relationship with someone who had become a drug addict, who never had any consistency to his behavior. Men said jump, I jumped. I thought this made me flexible when, actually, it cost me my spine. I wasn't flexible. I was a carcass.

However, I was a carcass having regular orgasms, which made things confusing. Ben would arrive at my tiny studio at 1:30 p.m. or 4:00 a.m. or whenever the hell he decided he wanted to come over, and I let him in my bed to do some of his best work. In retrospect, I probably should have been suspicious of someone who was so good at sex. As a twenty-three-year-old who had only ever been intimate with a couple people—one being existential-panic-sex on the evening after my college graduation (shout out to Quinn!)—I didn't know what was possible. I loved the feeling of suddenly being along for the ride, just totally dominated with pleasure and raw energy, even if it meant I wasn't in control. In fact, I loved not being in control. If I got up in the middle of the night to get water or pee, and I happened to press into him while climbing back into bed, that was all it took; he'd be on top of me, kissing my neck, insisting we fuck again. He called it that; he called it "fucking." And that's what it was.

In the mornings, we'd pull out oil pastels and large swaths of butcher paper and drink coffee and make art in our bathrobes, talking about the Tao Te Ching. I felt basic in the very best way. The sex was messing with my head, as were the late nights and the super-intriguing conversations about the "fascism of monogamy" and probably the paint fumes (occupational hazard) of being with a Real Ar-teest. The conversations about monogamy were benign enough, at first. At various potlucks with his circle of friends someone or other would bring up the concept of polyamory and how they loved the experience of having multiple partners at the same time. Looking back, there was a very clear distinction in these conversations: some, mostly with women, concentrated around the fact polyamory was a form of conscious rebellion against patriarchal standards. *It puts the power back in our hands*, they would exhale, before taking another deep drag on their spliff. *It forces a higher standard of communication. It takes the pressure off of the dyad. It's punk rock. It's art.*

And then there were the other conversations. Mostly with men. Most of whom had recently acquired a copy of the aforementioned *Sex at Dawn*, which—despite being a brilliant academic text—will always make me shudder as I remember the way these ~~scared little boys~~ males butchered the book's core argument that "humans aren't monogamous mammals" to justify why they had fucked your roommate. They would tell us it was better to be in the "flow of life and follow our natural urges"—i.e., someone, anyone, walks by in a tight shirt—than be restricted by rules and expectations. I lapped it up. And continued to, until Ben's according-to-him-but-not-according-to-her ex-girlfriend messaged me on Facebook[7] telling me she and Ben were very much together and, also, she had chlamydia, and I should probably get tested.

---

7. On Thanksgiving. For some reason, this made me feel extra shitty. Turkey AND the realization your lover is a total d-bag, and you've pissed off someone you don't even know? Just give it the weekend, geez.

Hooray! How positively Bohemian. Now, I not only had a not-boyfriend who refused to show me his house and always responded to calls with a text—I was ALSO potentially harboring my very own venereal disease. Did they talk about this in *Sex at Dawn*? If so, I didn't read it.

Turns out I didn't have chlamydia. I did, however, have one excruciatingly long conversation with the Other Woman (who was actually the original woman) in her place of business, which was a small dress shop. I agreed to meet her there to talk and, when I walked in, she locked the door behind us. I didn't know an adorable five-foot-three blonde woman who canned her own peach preserves could be menacing, but there you go. I learned a lot in my twenties.

I left that day feeling scalded but didn't stop there—oh no! That would be too simple. After that little visit to the dress shop, I confronted Ben (who largely denied it, claimed to be working through some things, he was just so free-spirited, have you studied Buddhism?, etc., etc.) and attended the music and arts festival he co-produced (ar-teest!) the following month. Within twenty-four hours, we were having unprotected sex in my tent because we had both been "tested" and were "on this journey together." Within forty-eight hours, my car battery had died, and Ben suggested his "friend" (who I knew from our delicious convo in the dress shop) use her car to jump mine, who I then learned was *also* having unprotected sex with him in *her* tent.

I wish I felt stupider. I honestly do. But my brain was wedged so far up my vagina at that point I don't even know if I could have located it if I tried. As she delivered the harsh news—she was very much NOT Ben's ex and very much NOT giving up—this lovely woman also chose to point out my skin was looking a little parched.

"Do you want some jojoba oil? You're so *scaly*," she added, teeth glinting.

I'd never been negged[8] by a hippie goddess before, but there's a first time for everything, I guess.

My car battery recovered, but it would be years before my feeling of self-worth did. I would visit Ben's bed—which felt like an accomplishment because it meant I was first string! I made it to HIS HOUSE!—several times over the next few months, each time losing a little bit more of myself in the sheets. And no longer in a good way.

It wasn't until one night when I brought a friend over and all three of us lay on the bed watching a movie. I was behind him (claiming my place?) while he spooned her. He eventually creeped his hands over the lip of her jeans and into her underwear . . . what the actual fuck? . . . and I FINALLY reached my limit. "Oh my *God,*" I screeched, leaping up from the bed like I'd just been burned. I had.

"Want me to call you an Uber?" he asked, casually grabbing a yogurt from the fridge.

Years later, I heard through the grapevine he had gotten his sometimes-girlfriend pregnant. I knew within minutes they would end up having a girl, and that he would have to see things from a new perspective, and this would all come around eventually. I took him to a ramen dinner and told him just as much. As it turns out, I had no idea just what life had in store for him, and to say he "learned his lesson" feels trite in the face of his life's many hardships and intricacies. But I still see him now and then, and we exchange pleasantries (which is easier to do when he's not trying to fuck you), and I wish him well. And I usually mean it.

⌒

---

8. A shitty comment disguised as a compliment, designed to make that person feel inferior (yet oddly beholden) to you. Shout out to jojoba oil, though. Jojoba has no fault here.

I still get confused, sometimes, about Ben's strange power over me. Or the man who came next, who I met at a drum circle, who invited himself to my birthday and stayed for the nonexistent after-party because he wanted to give me a "sound bath." What is a sound bath, you ask? Well, it's when a bearded man in sandals places an assortment of beautiful yet empty crystal bowls (are you there, metaphor? It's me, Jenna!) on the floor and plays them with a small wand and a lot of self-importance. Any time I have been in a sound bath I have almost immediately fallen asleep, including this time. I did NOT, however, fall asleep when the beardy sound man—his name was actually Casey—came over one week later, and we started making out, and he began taking off my clothes. I asked him if he had a condom, and I might as well have asked if he had a ten-year plan and a 401k.

"*No,*" he hissed, jumping back from me with clear disdain. I told him that I was not willing to have sex without one (I'd learned at least something by that point), and he seemed disgusted.

"I just thought you were more—more—*pure* than that," he said, curling up in my zinnia-print sheets and hugging his knees into his chest. If only he'd brought his sound bowls to take the edge off this obvious disappointment at my character.

Pure? *Pure?* In what universe of bead-wearing, yoga-practicing, bullshit male toxicity had it become *not pure* to want to avoid an STI with someone I barely knew? If I had meditated more, would I have simply been able to clear my vagina—sorry, YONI—from any disease or infection or emotional harm? If I visualized a wave of rainbow ponies flying between our bodies, would I have been okay with yet one more person co-opting my own spiritual curiosity—my desire to be more open—in order to manipulate me? Did he even know what he was doing or was he just all unexpressed sperm and appropriated Zen tattoos at that point?

For once, I made the right choice. I left Casey in my little bed and drove to a friend's house, where I slept on the couch. I didn't even care if he stayed in my studio. What would he take that he hadn't already threatened to? I returned the next day and washed my zinnia sheets in boiling water. Twice. And I never saw Casey again except a brief grocery store run-in a few years later wherein he informed me he thought my dad and I were probably aliens. What a good egg!

When I really examine my choice to submit to the spiritual fuckboi, or all the ways they informed my dating life and sense of self, I come across two options. One is to question my sanity, beat myself up for making dumb decisions, and be grateful I got out alive. The other is to look—to really wonder—at what it is I thought they promised me, forgive myself for not knowing it couldn't be given by someone else, and be grateful I got out alive.

I wanted to feel free. I'd spent my whole life up to that point feeling restricted within my skin and within my concept of what relationships had to look like. When I returned to the States after living abroad, something had unfurled within me; suddenly, I was drawn to men who seemed like they were free, like they were *really living* and not bound within the coils of conservatism. In short, they weren't being a Good Girl. And when I decided not to be one either, when I abandoned my standards and needs, I believed I was freeing myself—but what I really did was climb into a new box, take off my shirt, and wait to be manipulated in the service of someone else's sovereignty. Namaste, amiright?

Years passed and relationships came and went. They mostly came. I mostly went. I entered into the first truly healthy, adult relationship of my life, and my era of fucking the spiritual fuckboi became a distant spot on the horizon; I'd still see them, sometimes, in line at the juice bar or showing their "spiritually channeled" artwork at a beach gallery. I'd wave and smile. I had found a man who was interested in Buddhism, but could say things like "intersectional feminism" without gagging, and who didn't play games with my heart or head. I was grateful but still partially detoxing, and it was a full two years into my relationship before I realized just what that could look like.

Fast forward to May 2019, and I took the train down to LA to join my best friend in watching a very important cultural phenomenon—the Eurovision Song Contest[9]—from one of the best places to watch and best places in general: a gay dive bar. After several rounds of Stella Artois and many, many standing-room-only rounds of applause for the NEWEST LATVIAN SENSATION, and a surprise visit from my boy-friend's super-cool LA cousins, we finally made our way out into the day—squinting against the harsh 11:30 a.m. light—and proceeded to walk toward a wine bar. After all, we'd broken the seal. Eurovision is like the World Cup for theater kids: once a year, we need to drink, yell, and cry in the company of one hundred sweaty strangers before breakfast. We had done just that. And now, we had two options: go home and sleep it off or keep drinking, eventually order pizza, pull out the tarot cards, and pass out at the perfectly respectable hour of 5:15 p.m. We chose the latter.

Now: it is important to note we had only just arrived at the bar. We had barely put down our things, settled into the

---

9. Imagine the drunk uncle who you actually like to talk to, combined with the Ice Capades, combined with dry ice, combined with David Bowie: the cocaine years, combined with *the actual best music you've heard in a long time.* That's Eurovision. And goats, somehow? There're probably going to be goats.

overstuffed porch furniture, and I had ONLY just made my way to the bathroom—humming something in a language I don't speak—when they joined. By the time I walked out of the bathroom, one of them had their arm draped on the bench behind Shannon, and the other was perusing the chalkboard of wine specials; his hemp pants were folded over at the seam revealing a perfect trail of dark hair—like a neon arrow of doom—toward his pubic bone, and his artfully-distressed linen shirt was open just one button too many. I approached with caution. Suddenly, I overheard the first man—let's call him Dustin—asking Shannon about her mindfulness practice. You know, casual stuff. And before she could finish her answer, Dustin interrupted:

"Cool, cool. Yeah. That's cool. Actually, Scott and I meditate."

It took me thirty full seconds to realize this man—a stranger with zero qualms about sitting down, uninvited, to a rare gathering of female friends, whose body language was the equivalent of lounging on the couch in tighty-whities and eating cereal out of the box while his wife vacuumed around him—was *hitting* on her. It was a *LINE*. He had asked her a leading question in order to segue to what he had pre-determined to be his Most Fuckable™ quality: a mindfulness app that told him to breathe in, breathe out, breathe in, breathe out while wind chimes clanged in the background. He meditates. Scott also meditates. And together they so perfectly represented the kind of self-delineated evolved man I had spent the past ten years dating—so perfectly inhabited, with their frayed Birkenstock sandals and $400 leather watches, the exact breed of self-congratulatory hippie-crite I had finally escaped—that I burst out laughing. I couldn't help it.

Five years prior, I probably would have hung on his every word. I would have asked Scott how he meditated. Instead, I felt joy at knowing I could listen, could observe, without owing him anything. Not my time, not my body, not an explanation for why I would gladly choose watching reruns of *Bachelor in Paradise* over self-actualization.[10] Not one thing.

It took me a lot of time, and a lot of consensual participation in it, to be able to finally walk away from this shitty dynamic. I took a lot of liberties in typecasting these men; that is true. AND. That feels like an even trade for the years of my life, years I will never get back, where they did the same to me—hollowing me out, viewing me only as someone who would possibly affirm them. Worship them. Fulfill their time by giving my attention, my most valuable currency, without complaint or expectation of anything more than an occasional 1:00 a.m. text: *U awake?*

No, should have been my answer. No!

No.

And neither are you.

---

10. I would argue that this IS self-actualization. Feel free to disagree.

Occupy

My name is Jenna Nicole Tico.
Jenna, Nicole. Light, fair. A feminine variant on victory.
Tico, a masculine variant of Costa Rican.
A place I haven't been, but where the air bleeds warm, and they do yoga on the beach, and I'm told I will finally be free of you.

I am a white cis-woman born in central Chumash territory that we call Santa Barbara. Some of my ancestors were settlers on this land, and some of them weren't.
I carry blood from Ireland, Russia, Norway, and Spain, and in public, I am typically identified as heterosexual.

I am a visitor. A borrower. A moment of borrowed time.

I am a daughter, a stepsister, a lover, and a friend.
I am a reader of stories, a dreamer of sharks, and a person who eats on the couch.
I buy socks bearing flowers that only shoes see, and I've read books about the heteropatriarchy.
I have paid for people to file my nails.
I make art, I make out, and I've made up 233 excuses to get out of this story.

So please, tell me: of all the things I call myself—why do I still pick you out of a lineup?

Why—when, face-to-face with a checkbox that says "MAKE ME YOURS," do I still default to the one they won't print— the one that says,

"Abusive relationship: He didn't hit me,
But his cruelty made me feel real."

Because only someone who knew me that *well* could possibly hate All the same things I loved.

And only someone who *really* saw me Could disappear me so hard.

I've spent two years grappling with your ghost, and haven't spent one moment wishing you'd come back to flesh. Even in those small moments, When my own flesh grew cold, And I remembered your hand, And remembered its touch, And buried myself in the memory of your shoulder, just to not have to look at your face— Even then, I had to raise my own cheeks to the sun, Feel them burn every time I knew something was wrong, That it couldn't possibly be this hard to be seen By anyone other than you.

I dragged my lips against each insecurity, Feeling it alter my veins With the hint of a poem I could read in the dark:

This is who we were, this is how we loved.

And wondering how I could alter the words
To maintain that you made me invisible.

I've spent two years reading spiritual doctrine,
Taking walks in the sand, waking up with the sunrise
Like Oprah would do,
Learning how to make food that my ancestors probably stole
To keep warm, or impress a cute boy.
I have spent this time learning to clean my own heart,
And I track my ovulation
Just like Oprah would do.

And still, I am left with more questions than comments
And dozens of magazine quizzes that make me wonder just
how it is
That anyone manages to be in relationship?
We didn't do it right, baby, and now your shadow creeps on
me every time I get close
To the edge of my seat.

I'm with someone new now, and no closer to knowing
Just how it is
Two people can be separate and together at the same time.
One and still not the same.
But *Cosmo* tells me we can't share an apartment 'til I figure
it out.
And the cosmos warn me I'd better shed this last bit of you
Before opening any more dresser drawers
To all of the love he can hold.

And now you're back, and you want me to lubricate your
social joints as you plant your flag in a field of poor memories,
Waving an unwavering commitment to awkwardness—
And in it, commitment.

That precocious word
That no matter what I did,
Was never said, nor heard.

And then I think, maybe. Maybe I'm not meant to lose
Every scar you carved in my being.

And it's like that song, you know— "Because of You,"
I now know those notches completely.

Because of you, my body
Is the only thing I'm certain I am.

My body, the place you would turn away from
On the same horizontal plane, losing me in the particular kind
of silence
That only withdrawal can make.

Because of you, I see every momentary lapse in attention
As a moment to tear out my mind,
And every time I see foreign eyes
Occupy a familiar socket,
I remember how I finally left—adrenalized, cold,
Two swollen minutes that could have been twenty
Where you took your second-to-last bow.

But because of you, I know not to pick at the scab that says
I couldn't exist after dark.
I don't turn away when my past self balls up her fists
And believes even screaming won't work.

Because of you. You, who came through like a colonial un-set-
tler of my peace of mind
Piece of land that was stripped from my mother,

Like the truth that slipped as I swam to this Earth, entering
and forgetting and then re-membering in certain moments,
Like when art comes alive
For the first time, just like that first time when my feet walked
away from you,
The very first time they could,
And not a single moment sooner.

And now I am here. Mother, daughter, sister, wife.
Oops.
Daughter, friend, survivor, life.
I am held by my father and the blood of this Earth, and I have
friends who drive hours to see me. I am a college graduate
with cards that buy food and, when needed, can paint a whole
house. And. I still walked into the word that YOU hid from to
blur your own deeds; walked in like three blondes walk into
a bar—smearing sounds, the butt of jokes, losing everything.
I have enough self-esteem to fill up ten cups,
and still, I walked into our relationship willingly,
and STILL, I call it abuse.

And in the stillness that time has made whole, I have learned
to let some things go loose.
Like an old sweater, tufting in finicky colors that bunch at my
elbows and waist.
Like the kind of thing that I've always loved—always, a place
before you were born.

That knows you cannot own the harvest,
And you never saw me warm.

So how do we end? In real time, honey,
In the quiet moments that make sense of the pain.
I used to think that they wanted forgiveness,

But now, I only listen to them, patiently.
Like children,
Like smoke,
Like a window is there for the rain.

Like so many men in your lineage, you thought you could
keep what you could find.

But you don't.
You never did.
You never will.

Because it's mine.

To the New Girlfriend of the Man I Used to Blame for Nearly Everything

Hey, girl.

Do you mind if I call you girl? I dunno, maybe it would be better if I start with woman.

Hey, woman.

No, that sounds weird.

I'm not really sure what to call you, or say to you, or how to say it, because you're not sitting here with me. And if you were, I'd probably just be analyzing your eyebrows, and then wondering how my own face looks, and then saying something uncomfortable to pass the time. Kind of like this:

Do you know how hard it is to stalk you on the internet?

I'm not saying you should adjust your settings or anything creepy like that. Only that I stared at your Instagram profile pic for quite some time in order to determine if your expression looked like you are married or not. Married to the man who we share in common—whose energy, words, and juices have flowed through both our bodies.

Ew, gross, I know. And totally—yours way more than mine. For sure! You can totally have his juices. Sorry I said "juices."

But—you know how water has memory? Well, tissues have it, too. And mine are still peppered—and in some cases, livid—with the splintered ice he left behind.

Sorry, that was too much, too soon. You know how he has that weird thing his eyebrow does when he's thinking—but it makes him look super mad? So funny!

Yeah, it took me a long time to realize he was, in fact, super mad. That the very fact of my personality made him angry. What drew him to me—my close family, my colorful clothes, my creativity—were the same things he would try to destroy. Perhaps without even realizing it. And no, I'm not being dramatic. I'm telling the truth. And I'm telling you because I think you can handle it.

I don't know you, it's true.

But I worry about you, you know. In that same tiny photo I look at to wonder if you're married, I also scan your eyes for signs of distress. Does it keep you up at night, wondering if he will leave without saying goodbye? Does he throw things across the room when you forget to buy laundry detergent? Does he wait until he's inside of you, breathing over your face with his dark, distant eyes, to tell you he wants you—and from the way he says it, you can tell he really means to *own* you?

I remember the first time I saw him. As it turns out, it was an event totally out of his normal routine, a Christmas potluck, and I mistook it for regular. I saw him in his becoming, in his reaching. I didn't know that he'd never get to the place he showed me he wanted. At least, not in front of me.

He projected to me someone who was open. Seeking. Bathed in light. And we talked, and I lied about how old I was, which was one of the first signs I was in trouble. I wanted to be older for him, for him to see me as romantically mature. Because with him, I never wanted to be friends. In later years, he would tell me the first time he saw me, he thought about having sex with me. And I took it as a compliment.

Just checking, are you still with me? Ok, good. Because you drifted for a second there.

I just want to make sure you're okay.

What's that? Am I okay?

I'm not sure, to be honest. I mean, I am. I've moved on. I've moved so far on that I don't think of him that often; I don't even wonder if he's in a good mood and if that means we are all allowed to be in a good mood. Sometimes, I will still look to other people to tell me whether I'm allowed to be happy. He did that to me. He never hit me, but he tried to disappear me. He disappeared my happiness by making it contingent on whether he felt good in himself, which he hardly ever was, but he tried, so I was supposed to be okay with that, supposed to be okay with the trying.

I don't think of him that often.

But I do think of you. I wonder if you have been able to go this long without seeing that side of him, the one that gets angry without warning, the one that looks through your phone and decides you've dated every person you have a photo of; that you must be cheating on him, when he is the one who is repeatedly, decidedly fucking other people.

You must have seen some of the sides by now. Right?

Because you have to know, it predates you. It predates him, even. He was only doing what he learned. He wanted so badly to break the cycle. He wanted to, but didn't. He tried. He didn't try hard enough. Or did he?

Is he?

I certainly hope so.

I want to imagine you two thriving together, surrounded by other people who know the fullness of you—and him—who aren't afraid, who don't hide. I don't want him to hide you. I don't want YOU to hide. I want to imagine you eating. Eating sandwiches dripping with sauces and fresh tomatoes and the juices of delicious meat; food that will nourish you, feed you, help you grow. You see, I was always trying to shrink. It wasn't that I tried to stop eating. It was just I never had an appetite. I was always so afraid. Afraid of offending him, saying the wrong thing—doing the wrong thing, picking up the glass the wrong way, making the wrong comment—and my stomach was in knots. It's hard to eat the things thick with flavor when, deep down, you know your soul is being eaten by someone who doesn't even want it.

So are you eating? Do you have a job? I hope you have a job, and that he is supportive.

Have you brought up feminism? What did he say? Good god, woman—*what did he say?*

Because I remember.

You'll notice me wanting the best for you. Isn't that interesting? I don't want to pat myself on the back or anything, but it has definitely taken me a lot of therapy to be here. And I almost mean it! I'm like 85 percent there. The other 15 percent is spent worrying he is telling you your job is stupid, or you're stupid, or that you trust him to tell you whether you are good or not. The other part is worried that if he looks at you with disgust, you will believe him.

I know I did.

I probably could have loved him more. That's what he needed, after all. Someone who loved him the way his parents couldn't, because of their own stupid shit. Someone who loved him for something other than his face or his abs. Someone who saw his shit and made him want to do better, instead of growing afraid and then pushing it all away. It is very, very hard to love someone who you are so deeply afraid of. I didn't know that until later. But I know, and I knew, he needed someone to love him. I know, in hiding and lying and being otherwise terrified of him, I reinforced his worst fear. I couldn't be the one to do it, to love him the way he needed to be loved, when he didn't love himself.

So is it you? Have you cracked the code?
Does he speak to other people's wives the same way he speaks to single women?

I ask because I often wonder about that. Like, the way we only show parts of ourselves to certain people. He always showed the good part of himself—which I saw, pinky swear!—to women who were married to his friends. And his friends . . . well, I have to believe they had no idea. I have to. They saw someone charismatic, philosophical, athletic, smart. Convincing. Like Harold Hill, but without the tubas.

Oh sorry, are you too young and/or cool to get that reference? My bad. I'll bring it back on track.

It's just, like: I think he saved those parts of himself, the ugly parts, for me—and maybe for you, I'm not sure—because he was probably tired of having to always keep up appearances. I'm sure it exhausted him. And when we're around the people we really love, or really know, we tend to show the full spectrum—to really take it all off. Like losing your bra at the end of a workday. I think the good parts were kind of a bra. With me, he just let it all hang out. Picturing him like that, like someone who was just doing his best, often helps me.

Was I supposed to feel lucky I was the only one seeing the full picture? Do you see it now? And do you feel lucky?

Gosh. I just don't know.

I often wonder what terrible things you must have heard about me. I know I heard it all, about all of the others—and even though I thought it was weird, I was too busy wanting to impress him. But the way he always talked about other women—the ones he had dated seriously—like they were always the problem. Always *crazy*. I'm sure I'm the crazy one now.

And maybe I am.

I'm good with that, honestly. If I have multiple heads or if I'm carrying multiple heads in my hands—all dripping with blood, from where I've cut off his personalities, or seen through them, simply knew too much—I am not surprised. It's my legs, really, that I'm worried about. In your image of me, do I have legs? Was I able to run?

I wanted to run. But instead, I sat in my flannel robe, glued to the floor. Crying. Refreshing Facebook to see if he had messaged me. For any sign of life, inner or outer.

I don't deny he believes he was right. After all, he felt strong emotions, and those emotions were real. He was mad. He was sad. And if the feeling is strong enough, we can all convince ourselves of their cause. That we must be right about how we were wronged.

But, my dear, if you need to hear this—or if anyone does—I'll just leave this here:

It's okay to feel like the one who was wronged.

And it's okay to find a way to feel good again.

For me, feeling good meant getting out. After all, I was in deep. And we made a habit in our relationship of poking one another in our deepest, most karmic wounds. Imagine if we had just been honest with each other! I lied to him because it wasn't safe to tell the truth. But I hope that has changed now. We didn't have the tools, but I hope you do. I really do.

And most of the time, I want the best for him. That's true too.

Everyone thinks they will be the one to be able to spot it. That they'd see abuse heading toward them like a four-wheeler, gas guzzler, honking at a hundred miles per hour. The truth is—and I'm done lying now—sometimes it's more subtle. Sometimes we don't see it coming. Or sometimes we do, and we walk toward it anyway. Because it's pretty. Or because we still need healing and learning.

Maybe both.

I know I began to doubt myself as a result of being with him—and that was the toughest spell of all to break. I doubted my own instinct and my own ability to call out when something wasn't right. In my current work, I rely on this instinct daily. And sometimes, I think of him. And I thank him, silently, for what he taught me. For what he broke in me, and how it grew back in me stronger. More dialed. More clear.

Being an intelligent person is no protection. I wish someone had told me, warned me.

Anyhow.

I hope it's okay I'm sharing all of this. If it's not, you can always tell me. I hope your voice is strong. And your resolve. I hope when you lie face down on the bed that he rubs the knots out of your back and that he didn't put them there—and when you flip over, your whole underbelly showing, that you feel safe.

Loved.

It seems to me that, in some alternate space time reality, you and I might have been friends. Maybe we would have been in a book club or something, or swapped ideas, or sat next to one another at a comedy show and whispered about the things we both found funny. Maybe I'd always be studying you, in the way your eyes seem so open and yet so far away. I wonder if you'd hide behind your hair. If you'd let your guard down. Or if I would, for that matter.

After all, we share the same space, you and I. They say water has memory. The body does too. I know mine does. How long does it take for that shit to go away? For the DNA, the thousands of question marks, the would-be human combinations who are here to solve—to maybe finally free—the karma like a combination lock. Sometimes I wonder if we could have talked about that. If, on another desert, in another time and place, we could approach one another across the quaking sand—hold delicate fingers to one another's cheeks, and feel hot, swollen tears slip down from the place where we both know we've seen it too much, and seen it too much to stay quiet. I wish I could ask you, not in pieces, but in one whole: *are you safe in there?*

I'm not really sure how to wrap this up. This is a little awkward now, I guess.

But we will get through it.

And so will you. I see that now.

Just like the part of him still living in me, and the part of me that probably still exists in him. It's a trade, you know. It always is. And I'm okay with that. I hope he got my better, kinder parts. I hope I got his.

I hope we all get something. Other than the lonely parts, the broken parts; the hundreds of thousands of strands of DNA, who could have become little boys, who could become brave men, who could maybe break the cycle. Who almost became someone. Who just wanted to become someone good.

Love,
Jenna

Other People I Can Blame

1. My high school boyfriend
2. Myself
3. My mother
4. No one

High

I don't want to talk about him.

I don't want to talk about the fact he arrived at the exact moment my guard was down, walking home from the high school at the start of a four-day weekend, with a red and pink tank layered over my t-shirt for Valentine's Day, or the note he had left on the porch of my mom's house. I didn't even know it was from him, except I did, because there was no one else. I don't want to talk about the fact that for five years afterward there was no one else. Not even me. Especially not me.

I don't want to talk about the way he bled into my brain, consuming my thoughts during the day and especially into the night, and how he showed up at unexpected times to take me on walks to the mountains, the beach, or the hilly slope behind the high school. How we would talk for hours and how the first time we kissed there was classical music playing in the background; he gave me the key to a snare drum like it was the key to his heart, which it was, and also to his unraveling. I don't want to talk about the fact that he cut into his own flesh that weekend and dipped his young man's lips into the blood in order to make a red kiss onto a piece of paper for me, a piece of his DNA to carry with me always. Which I would, like a promise, like a pledge, like a prayer we would one day return to those early times on the roof at sunset; tears pouring out of his eyes, out of mine, briny liquid flooding my stomach and my cotton underwear as we walked up the stairs to his aunt's house, and he said he loved me, and he entered me, and no one had ever entered me before, and we enveloped one another completely.

I don't want to talk about how good it was; when it was good. How we would make promises to one another of our grandchildren; talked about how they would look at photos, both of us forgetting we had to survive in order for them to exist. I don't want to talk about the late nights in his childhood room, hours spent tracing the outline of each other's bodies with fingertips like brushed flannel, enveloped in the completeness of first love and sexual awakening; how every single sense was electrified into neon colors of wonder, possibility, thirst. I don't want to talk about the way his eyes shivered as he slept, someone sleeping next to me, which had never happened before. About the long journeys in his white truck, holding each other's bodies within our mouths like a game, like candy, and pulling over to look at the sunrise, pausing only to sleep, but never fully sleeping; so awake, so alive, so impossibly together. I don't want to talk about the notes he left me, consumed with me, how it couldn't sustain, how the flame went out on the Bunsen burner each night, how little I thought about what could possibly go wrong.

I don't want to talk about the years I spent watching him play music, watching him watch me watch him play music, how he always showed up two hours, four hours, ten hours later than we decided, walking into my dad's house smelling like sweat and Gatorade and other people's weed. I don't want to talk about the power heaving off his body while he sang, while he slammed the keys with all the ferocity of someone who could so gently love me each night as we went home, or the way he etched my name into the head of his drum, just begging others to see. I begged others to see.

I don't want to talk about the begging, how I waited at the foot of his bed like a creature enveloped in fire and longing, twisting my limbs like the knots in a tree as he laughed and clinked in the other room; music pouring out of him, love pouring out of me, like an incantation. I don't want to talk about the molding Persian rug, the groupies, the bags of stale chips and tables of ashtrays and guitar picks and promises. I don't want to talk about that stupid door and the way it slammed, or the lead singer's hair as it hid his face, and his truth, and the way we lost the thread. I don't want to talk about those summers at the house with the empty pool, and the guitarist who punched another man until his blood splattered against the parched concrete, or the way I knew something had to be wrong. Or the way our bodies always found each other at the end of a long day, or a week apart, or breaking up, or REALLY breaking up this time, only to come back together again. I don't want to talk about the band tours that came out of nowhere, that just had to happen, or the splintered plans, my splintered heart. I don't want to talk about it.

I don't want to talk about the years leading to the years at the end, the snake's tail eating itself, the time we spent running away up the California coast, or the way he would climb in my window to just be near my body, to leave me a love note, his muddy footprints visible for days. I don't want to talk about the way he did heroin with a beautiful girl while we were broken up, which I knew he would because he loved drugs, and he loved me, and one was not enough. I don't want to talk about the fact he told me I was too much, my feelings were too much, or how his voice took the place of the one inside my head, and how it berated me. How I spent years believing I was too much, too much, yet not enough. Not enough to keep him from taking the drugs, from hiding them inside his dresser drawer; not enough to keep me from looking for them, finding them, smelling their outline against the cold wood, crying. Too much to let go.

I don't want to talk about the time I caught him stealing pills from his grandmother's cabinet, and how I ran up the street—my eyes, my heart, a mess—discovering a boundary, finally, only to hear his feet coming up behind me. I don't want to talk about the way I turned around, or the way we held each other, his tears soaking through my scarf and straight through my resolve, and how we'd spend years doing this, exactly this; me loving him, him loving the drugs, him loving me, me being a drug, forever at an impasse. I don't want to talk about the hundreds of diary entries, the feeling of destiny, being unable to avoid one another but unable to stay apart; the thousands of lies, the millions of kisses, the catch-and-release of finally breaking free and then finding one another's bodies again. Our only real home. A fortress in the transition away from childhood. I don't want to talk about that. I don't want to talk about the way I would show up at his house, shaking and raw, to be enveloped in his scent, into the smell on his breath, knowing but not wanting to know, and letting him enter me. Like he had done that very first time. Like I knew I was meant to be felt—meant to be filled.

I don't want to talk about the postcards, the distance, the promises made and then broken. I don't want to talk about what I don't know, what I could never know. The twitching in the middle of the carpet. The way my own stomach betrayed me into vomiting, so many times, when I knew it just wasn't okay. Something wasn't okay. I don't want to talk about watching him smash his perfect, pink-cheeked face into his own fist, and then the wall, wanting to disintegrate himself, and I thought if only I could do it for him, if only I could dissolve, and so I tried. I don't want to talk about the way I wasn't right, how I knew and we all knew I wasn't right, and he wasn't right, but we did it anyway. Lips like magnets, like forever, like the mark on a board and a dart sped at miles and miles per hour, too fast to stop. Too fast to feel.

I don't want to talk about his tongue along my teeth, or the way he would hold the side of my jaw between his thumb and forefinger and tell me how he couldn't get enough of me. I don't want to get enough. I don't want to talk about never feeling like enough. I don't want to talk about his touch, his completeness, the language he spoke only I could understand, or the way I still hear him. I don't want to talk about the fact that, sometimes, I feel nothing. I don't want to talk about the fact that, sometimes, that's not true.

I don't want to talk about his arrest or the phone call I got while standing in someone else's kitchen, elbows digging into someone else's counter, in a different state, where he couldn't climb in my window, where I couldn't run into him at the store. I don't want to talk about the way my heart sank, and then swelled, and the memory of our phantom grandchildren; how they'd never live, but I would, I would live. And so would he. I don't want to talk about how he survived, or the hard work he did, or how I fantasized about being seen by him, casually elegant, years later, thriving. I don't want to talk about how he finally did see me, and we said hello, and how the wall came down, and I didn't feel afraid of him; worse, how I felt pity. I don't want to talk about sitting on the lip of my car, sobbing, listening to a friend say

one day,
you will find someone who makes you feel good,
instead of someone who makes you feel high.

I don't want to talk about how true that was. I don't want to talk about whether it broke me. I don't want to talk about hosting him in my living room, a reunion of old friends, eating a grilled cheese sandwich like it was nothing in the world, like I hadn't been naked in front of him more times than I could count, like he hadn't told me he would die without me. And here we were living our lives, living them with other people, unfazed.

I don't want to talk about how that felt. I don't want to talk about how it still feels, a decade later, to want to pick up the phone and say to him, *We did it, we survived! We didn't die!* And to know he won't answer, he won't pick up the phone; just like he didn't, he never did. I don't want to talk about the fact I'm better off without him. I don't want to talk about the indelible mark he made on my brain, in my heart, on the viewfinder I use for the most beautiful and terrible things. I don't want to imagine him happy. I don't want to imagine him sad. I don't want to see him aging, belly protruding, hair gray, hair that I used to pull within my teeth, eating it, eating myself, anything to be closer to him. How we crawled inside one another to stay sheltered, how we wanted it all, how we wanted everything. And how we lost it. How we got it all back. How we got more.

I don't want to talk about him, or the way we loved each other purely, fatally. I don't want to be strangers. I don't want to be friends.

I don't want to forget. I don't want to remember.

But I do anyway.

PART III:

Waxing

Vital

1.

Sometimes I see myself as a skeleton

Just a pile of spine

2. RESTING BLOOD PRESSURE: 90/60 MM/HG TO 120/80 MM/HG

What she should have told us was that she was dying *soon*. She was dying yesterday, and the day before that—dying while She measured hazelnut coffee onto a tablespoon, using Her toes to propel a rocking chair back and forth, back and forth, as She raised the hot liquid to her lips. Just because there are beep-beep-beeps coming out of Her does not mean She'll die any sooner than I am here, cross-legged, moving so fast (thousands of miles above the middle of the United States) I swear I'm not moving at all.

I'm looking at the man sitting across the airplane aisle: a mullet balances atop his head like a piece of raccoon that got tired on its way to the cockpit. I want to find a way to bring it up in conversation, to begin (perhaps) with the tiny star inked beneath his left eye and then find a way to touch his hair, because I'm overwhelmed by the feeling—at one point—he considered it to be a good idea. His wife is tracing her lack of eyebrow with what looks like a felt-tip marker. I want them to look at each other, for her to hold me in her torso like a cough and keep me there as the landing gear stammers out. I want to touch my cheek to her face and to the window, and I want to scream underwater until bubbles shoot out my nose.

3. BREATHING: 12-18 BREATHS PER MINUTE

A twenty-something from Seville seduces my friend and then phones his wife. My uncle drinks the mouthwash when he thinks no one is looking. Meanwhile, She is a surge protector at the center of a dozen beep-beep-beepings, small eyes staring forward and up like She can't believe She is the common denominator. Other than the connection between pencil and post-it, Her eyes are the only things that move. Four blue ones meet, and She drinks me in

Treasure tiny sips of water.

And when I say I will, I am lying. There is only something green that has the texture and temperature of vomit. While we stand in a circle, crying, my face is pressed into my mother's clavicle; a sharp pain flashes against my cheekbone, and I close my fingers around it. Finally, a pain that reveals itself FACE FIRST instead of the one crawling up through the box spring of a bed that I slept in as a child that smelled like summer at the beach and the sex I didn't even know I wanted to have and the idea that my neck was free,

would ever

I can understand.

My mother, suddenly a daughter, and an uncle who smells like a combination of Glade Plug-Ins and flood damage. I wish I could get up in the middle of the night

But I thought I wouldn't feel Her illness in my body until She was done with it.

4. PULSE: 60 - 100 BEATS PER MINUTE

Fade in on a girl eating cereal out of a flowerpot, hips resting against the sink, eyes focused on a point somewhere on the other side of the snow-crusted window. Actually, that's a lie—probably straight out of some TV show I pretend I don't watch. What I'm really doing is eating cereal out of a perfectly normal plastic bowl. With a fork. What are dreams except a Technicolor vision of what we think we've already seen, only minus the smell?

Pan to a hospital scene, beep-beep-beep, and a parade of saltine crackers lining the arm of a plasticky chair. It's my seventh hour here, and they still haven't touched Her feeding tube. Milky liquid pours out of the tracheotomy and onto Her chest, the same place I used to place my head. I think this thought, I eat it up, and am acutely aware The Melodrama has placed it there; not me, that it is not my thought, it belongs to this room and the fluorescent light buzzing overhead. But I swallow it anyway and wonder if airport security can smell broken hearts the way they can drugs and Gatorade. How much can they see with that x-ray machine?

I can see Her heartbeat beneath the cotton sheath on her chest. Thu-thump. Thu-thump.

Zoom in on a girl standing in the hall, phone pressed against her ear, hear with a melted face. It's absolutely unbelievable how long it takes someone to die; it's unbefuckinglievable with all the beep-beep-beeps and the nights spent awake and the diapers and the needles and the numb, the numb, when a relationship can end in the time it takes for tiny waves to travel from a phone in California to one in New Jersey. Roger that. The Melodrama throws its head back and cackles, because surely in this moment I am not alive, *How unfair, how horribly insensitive, how could this possibly have happened to YOU; what did YOU do to deserve this; WHO DOES THAT; how could this possibly, you won't make it, you won't make it, you won't.*

And much to my surprise, the floor does not open up and swallow me whole. My feet walk me back to Her hospital room, past Her roommate with the stain trickling down her starchy sheets and onto the floor, and Past. Present. Future.

5. TEMPERATURE: 97.8 - 99.1 DEGREES FAHRENHEIT / AVERAGE 98.6 DEGREES FAHRENHEIT

Optimist, pessimist, narcissist.

One, two, three.

There are different types of knowledge: the things you know, the things you know you don't know, and the things you don't know you don't
know. I've heard it said
That bad luck comes in threes.

I've muscled myself into this position

Optimist, pessimist, narcissist.

6.

Ding. Flight attendants, prepare for landing.

You feel things too strongly, like the delicate skin under your eyes. The mountains below look like veiny hands gripping onto California for dear life. You understand, quite suddenly, what alone feels like—grief is something you do alone. Losing someone is something only you do. There is more than one position for the neck and, sometimes, forward and up feels more like a whispered *ah* than a freeing of the head or back. The muscles lengthen and widen, but they do it in the weird half-place between sleeping and waking where you can't leave for fear you'll miss something. There's a feeling, just a feeling, and the engine hums beneath your spine; and your palms, they are wet. And the delicate skin under your eyes, it is wet.

A Surface that Breathes

Sleeplessness, like most things I avoid, is a fickle jerk. One moment, I'm walking upstairs—lit by the strange, bloodless buoyancy that so often accompanies exhaustion—and the next moment I'm in front of a bathroom mirror: blotchy, fluorescent, unreal. Here but not. Awake, but faded in random locations like a map that's been left in the sun.

I pick the stupidest times to stop drinking coffee. The spring of my senior year in college, days after my drug-addled boyfriend screeched out of the driveway—effectively ending our five-year relationship, though it would be another 435 days before I located the self-esteem to stop scanning each room for his voice—I sat down to work on my thesis, or one hundred pages of cryptic proof that I'd actually attended a lecture. Only one week earlier, my Nana had succumbed to a brief, astonishingly painful battle with cancer, and my family lay blown apart like children who have been blasted by a science experiment; eyebrows singed off, hair standing on end. Meanwhile, I'd sworn off caffeine, bread, and sugar, like a total self-indulgent hippie with a death wish. I waved at the world from my crater of grief, envying those I saw living with ease, using my health kick as means to simultaneously judge and pursue anyone who peered over the edge. "Let me get this straight," my friend sighed, forty minutes into one of our biweekly phone calls. "You just lost two of the most important people in your life, and you're writing this bitch of a paper all day every day. And you decided to give up coffee?"

Yes, I answered, running my mind over her choice of words: Lost. Like I'd somehow misplaced them, left them inside the deep folds of a couch. Then she snorted.

"Get *over* yourself." She laughed, voice inhabiting both corners of jolly and dark. "You'll be fine. But seriously, get over yourself. Drink some coffee. It's probably the best thing left in your life, other than me."

It should come as no surprise, then, that—several years later—I am on my fourth cup of the day, bookstore din pounding at my temples, with a new almost-boyfriend and a dead grandmother who is still dead and a thesis gathering dust on a shelf like a set of fine china, or second toaster. I say almost-boyfriend because that is what he is: if a boyfriend is one who shows up unannounced, he is the one my feet find in the dark. I call him because I don't need to. The "almost" is the part retracting in the night; that curls onto its side when its arm falls asleep; that doesn't find ways to keep touching. The "boyfriend" thing happens in places like this, large bookstores where candles go on clearance, where I pick up one labeled "Patchouli and Tobacco"—the way that his shirt pocket smells—and feel my organs collapse. Two weeks ago, I "almost" avoided caffeine, powering through the headache phase much like one grows out a bad haircut: fifty shades of mullet, all cowlicks and doubt. But then he pressed into my spine, spent an evening that lingered in maybes, and . . . well, I've abandoned my high horse, because fuck that shit, and am spinning about on a placemat set with hell, ablaze with the coffee and imperfect heaven and knowledge that soon it will fade. When it does, I'll most likely be standing here—still smelling a candle—wanting to cry, like a kid who's exhausted and can't reach the sink.

It's funny, the things we use to feel in control; beverage in, beverage out. Picking a font that Gen X hates. Tricking the brain into thinking "cool, now we're working" or "shit, I guess we're not." Meanwhile, the chair I'm sitting in has cracked from overuse, the leather spilling out beneath my white legs like a tired trampoline. To my right, a stack of books advertises the latest trends in staying healthy, boasting titles like *Wheat: Your Brain's Silent Killer*; which of course, makes no difference if everyone dies of Ebola.

So last night, my almost-boyfriend and I lay splayed with the TV set on, bouncing between red-and-white newscasts that broadcast the end of the world: epidemics, where to run in a landslide. Too dry and too hot; too wet, walls that spit mold into the air. A rattling cough in your lungs. Two channels away, a handful of Miami jerkoffs entered a tattoo salon and begged a girl with black hair to cover up their drunken mistakes; to make cuss words turn into alligators, so they can say, "Thank you, you've saved me. You've *saved* me. My God."

("Jerkoff," by the way, is a word my uncles use when attempting to distance themselves from the blight of humanity. For example, "that jerkoff cut me off at the intersection and made me spill my Big Gulp" or "I was talking to that chick, but some jerkoff came over and hit on her, so I put Visine in his beer.")

So these jerkoffs complained to the camera, and I flinched at the fact this word has made its way into my vocabulary—or at least into the part of my brain narrating late-night television. No matter the channel, the world was still going to shit; but in my world, the space around my face where I breathe in and out, there was only the pooling of head into chest. That, and the beat of his heart; so steady, so sure, no "almost." No, maybe. I let myself think perhaps this was all I'd been wanting; perhaps it's all anyone wants: just to give into gravity on top of a surface that breathes. To feel the consistency of life underneath and the soft electricity of someone else's fingers tracing over our valleys and peaks. The places where memory lives.

Earlier that night, we had sprawled on a thinly lit porch, our bodies still learning their blocking; your head here, my arm there, here is the spot where we take tiny air gulps. Someone's cigar smoke unfurled overhead like the branches of a tree, a flawless embodiment of ease.

"It's like the whole universe in microcosm," he uttered, watching the feathery stream dissipate, and I knew in that moment was a microcosm of the relationship as well: beautiful at its release, transient, perfect, always leaving. I watched the pieces of what we were creating, every word we'd decided to say, peel off into smoke. And I lay there later, head on his heartbeat, I could only feel: *Thank you.* Thank you, thank you, thank you, for not knowing your place, but for living despite it, and for teaching me the importance of making mistakes. They don't feel like mistakes when you're making them.

"I like you *now*," I told him quite suddenly, turning my face so it settled inside of his bubble.

"Not for who you were, or who you will be. Who you are. I like you now."

"Thank you." He laughed gently.

"You're welcome," I replied, more certain than I felt. At this, he exhaled a little too fast, letting out a small noise: almost as though it surprised him, my place in the order of things. That I'm someone who knows to say *Yes, I did this. On purpose.* And lying there, side-by-side, the universe ringleting over our heads, I think I surprised myself too.

Standing in line at the bookstore this morning, I had the option of ordering decaf. I had the option, as well, of walking into traffic with my backpack teetering precariously atop my stinging, sleep-deprived bones but, in the end, I'm taking a break from extremes. It's a choice to move forward, just as it is to kiss a boy in the car; and we save ourselves quietly, looking both ways at each light. By the time I finally put down the Patchouli candle, pushing my glasses up the bridge of my nose, where they sat—fogged with longing—to help me to see, my caffeine tuxedo had ripped at the seams. It's just me underneath it, warm skin and all: covered in bug bites that itch as I walk to the parking lot, tiny medals of appetite, the world's and my own. Feeling this, I climbed into the van of a man who calls himself my uncle, but is really just a man I met at an ecstatic dance in Austin. He immediately flicked on the radio and began to use the tops of his legs to drive while his hands darted around.

"Are you *flossing?*" I asked him, incredulous.

"Yeth," he replied, mouth full of fingers. "Does that bother you?"

"No," I answered. *Yes.*

"It's all about the knees," he told me, using his left one to steer. "I have periodontitis, so I floss every chance that I get.

"Do you floss?"

I touched my right hand to my lips, remembering the last time my dentist had asked that same question: to which I lied "Yes!" as a torrent of blood gushed from my gums.

"Not as often as I'd like," I replied. It's true: I'm on break from excuses.

As I opened my notebook to write *buy some floss* in small letters, right beneath the To-Do list that read "call your mother" and "bitch less," I realized I must have some faith in my life, to think about things like the fact my gums are receding. Just like somewhere, deep down, I know broken hearts must get healed. In a minute, I'll pick up the phone and dial my mom—even though phones remind me of brain cancer. I just have to; I have to tell her about the day I had yesterday, the tattoos, and the way the sun sets over warm Texas water.

But not 'til I finish my coffee. We wouldn't want it to get cold.

Elegy for the End of the World

It's strange, isn't it, to keep doing things? Sometimes.
When each day the news shows a "nation in crisis," and there's ninety-nine hundredths of the planet who don't even make it onto the television at the YMCA, but you're pretty sure they're in crisis, too. Another day and there are more children hurt, and your heart snaps in two.

But somehow you're still here. Doing things.
Pedaling at an exercise bicycle, punishing your knees up an invisible hill just to remind yourself that you're still beating, there's something worth beating; and at night, you will dab anti-aging cream beneath your eyes as if that is a thing that still needs to be done.
The world is heating up.

Is it okay, then, to still want to look up recipes for Chicken Marbella, plant sunflowers, and worry about electromagnetic waves —
Or learn how to pickle onions, just because it makes you feel like someone who does things?

Like the kind of person who pickles in mason jars, and plans
for a future where children are grateful for Chicken Marbella
and you are having chats with your friends over Chardonnay,
oh my belly, don't even get me started.

You turn to your belly each night, listening for gurgles or other
signs of life
The intricate chorus that rose like a tide, the one time that
woman touched you
"Transformational massage," she called it, digging into your
abdomen with expert fingertips
Saying things like *it's okay for me to be here, it's okay*
I choose this body
I am at home in this skin
When really, at best, it's like being a renter
In a building that's about to be tented for termites
For the rest of eternity.

Is it okay, then, to still want to tune into Netflix, wondering
just wondering what that one person will do next?
And who will she choose? Who will she choose?
WHO WILL SHE CHOOSE?

Or watch 45 minutes of African chimpanzees baring jagged
mouths of teeth.
Their home, this jungle laid out with vines and hierarchy, and
so many opportunities to get left behind
before you have the right feathers to get the grown ups' approval.
Africa, our shared home. The original
Mother who now sees us clearly
And says, *it's been grand, but get out of my house*
You've been leaving the toilet seat up and I'm done with it

The world isn't ending. The world will be fine.
We're the ones who have finally reached the limit

Of forgetting one another
Reached the bristling end of a rope bred in exile
Doing our downward facing dogs in the morning, protecting
our spines
And refusing to microwave our soup
Just in case it really is bad for us
Diligently protecting against unseen horrors
Because the ones we can see
Are just too much to bear

What was it like before we turned on the news
And heard one more reason not to fall asleep?
Perhaps it has always been this way,
Building homes on the edge of a knife
Just to whittle ourselves into someone who believes.
Perhaps there have always been children who learn to duck
and cover before they learn to cover their bases, and faceless
men we can't forget
Blowing holes in the vision we have for a future
Where we can still pick things up from the ground, and rub
them clean
Like a father polishing an apple against his cotton shirt for
his child to eat.

We laugh even as we talk about how we won't drink too much
coffee,
Like people have always done, wrapping their arms around
an invisible future
Where arm flab matters, and we want to sleep through the night.
Maybe you say you won't drink wine anymore,
Or at least not from California, where you heard they use so
many chemicals
That they light up our bodies on screens
And bear effervescent scans of toxicity.

Which is a relief, isn't it? The kind of toxicity that can be measured
Instead of the kind that runs beneath the threads that bind
us together,
Still holding us in a spiderweb of longing for better deals on
car insurance
Despite our best efforts
To split them into hairs.

"Someone has let it go bad," your grandma says
And you know she is talking about Las Vegas
But can't help but wonder if she's talking about all of it, too.

The world isn't ending. The world will be fine.
It will go on past the point where we've forgotten how to see
one another
Across the lines that someone told us we needed to stay
behind, would keep us apart
Past the point where we check for emergency exits,
Or stop making new babies to hold up to the light
Like we do with stained glass, or some other reminder of God.

Past the point where we brush against the fingers of a stranger
on the bus,
Both of us going in the same direction
Toward an arrival that still feels like too much
And we ignore the impulse to twine, flesh to flesh
For just one moment longer than could seem like an accident.

But the world isn't ending. The world will be fine.
It's the death of the promise, dangling the invisible weight of
not wanting to plan
For a world that won't promise to take care of our babies.
Which maybe it never did.

And maybe the most we can do is
Touch one another in order to survive.
Brush against a stranger's hands, and squeeze our cheeks
together in front of the mirror like a prayer
For deeper wrinkles
For the chance to have a face, and a body that has crinkled
from good use

To yowl each night toward
The same navy carpet of oblivion, and also, monotony. More
laundry to fold.
And to the person sitting next to you on the bus, as frozen
in time
As the newspaper open on her lap, catching your eye with a
headline, *ENOUGH*—
You curl together, into one tiny, naked need.
Wordless.
Worldless.

And the need to notice
Parallel in the invisible aliveness that binds you
To agree at least—
            That no matter what, you will move at the light.

Segue:
Are You Okay in There?

I still feel you there, in my hand.

Sorry if it's gone a bit sweaty.

Outer Space: A Play in Four Acts

OPENING

You dream of yourself at a former age — maybe ten years ago — when you still had a bit more flesh around your cheeks, at the sides of your breasts, and in other places where childhood gets trapped. You see yourself in a long, silk skirt, or some other thing you might have worn at the time, and let your gaze travel upward to your hair — more coiffed than usual, this being a dream. Then, with karate-like precision, you drive a stake the size of a pole vault through the heart of your younger self and watch as cherry-red blood spurts from the sides of her body.

Her expression, strangely enough, remains calm. (In dreams, you can die and still be relatively unfazed.) You wait for a message to arrive from above, something to indicate the pain is over. You have done what you needed to do, like a penance, and now your romantic relationship will return to what it was before. Not back to normal because it never was. (Normal does not sit on the same continent as the light between your smiles.) But it'll be back and, so will he.

You blink your eyes open, half expecting the sun. But it's gone, and so is he.

And you're not smiling. He wasn't smiling when you asked in the night: *What's going on?* You were lying on your back, tears streaming down the sides of your face and pooling in your ears. It was the first introduction of doubt. Up until this point, the two of you had been blissfully—almost supernaturally—in love; and if ever there was a moment of hesitation, it did not carry the seven-ton nametag: "HELLO, my name is Doubt." And it's not even doubt in the other, but doubt in yourself: in your own ability to maintain something untamable. The kind of love you always dreamed of. And with it, a commitment that needs more than a snuggle to survive. A relationship that needs, that MUST take, healthy space in order to survive. A reserve of inner wealth who knows—believes— he will return.

But he heard your question, and then turned his back and said, "nothing's going on" with a tone you swore you'd heard before, but never on him, and it spooked you. To the core.

No relationship stays in Eden forever. Yet faced with the crossroads, the Take-Four-Days-Apart or watch it all fall apart; you weren't expecting to slide to the kitchen floor so quickly where the memory, now stored in your molars, can only repeat like a drum.

"Why don't you want to see me, or speak to me, for four days?"
"Why

    don't

        you

            want   ~~to see~~

                me

           ~~or speak to me, for four days~~

                      ?"

You carve "spring renewal" out of the script somewhere, but, between the lines, there is only a slab of grief: grief for the relationship that didn't know phone silences, didn't need to take days to need one another; and most of all, for the girl who you so recently stabbed through the heart. The one who couldn't understand another person's honest request for space. She knew all along she couldn't come with you into the next part. She knew, but couldn't tell you. Couldn't bear to let you know you'd have to begin it alone.

I. ACT ONE

Four days?

Who needs four DAYS??

It's longer than you thought; has burst the bubble you made for yourself to float in, Glinda-style, above everyone else, singing, "I am a mature, confident adult!" as you agree to exactly three days of silence. Almost as though it were your idea. Three days is the plot you prematurely signed off on. But then your boyfriend, the one who you know you want to be with; he asked for four days to clear his head, because he has grown weary of your spray hose emotions. He loves you, and he wants to be present for your emotions without feeling you take them out on him. He needs space. And you shatter. Four minutes is more than you thought you could bear. Four hours is enough to miss him completely, to have to face all four directions of yourself, which—to be honest—you'd rather not do.

Four words:

I love you, but

Four more:

You're breaking my heart

And now you're lost in a cosmic, stomach-swirling storm of wondering how many of his friends are judging you, casting a shadow on your perfect love, all because no one ever taught you how to grow up.

And growing up is fucking brutal.

You recall an instance just a few nights ago, where you told him a story as he struggled to fall asleep: the invention of fairies came from the first time a child's heart broke. In *Peter Pan*, fairies are born from the first laugh, and somehow you know as soon as the child in the story looked into his mother's eyes—saw her laughing—he also saw her clearly for the first time. His mother, a person who knows to adore something purely is to already know it will end. Out of that came fairies.

Out of this comes you. But not yet. It's still night.

Out of night comes yogurt. Lots of yogurt, eaten after 11:00 p.m., for no reason other than it is the only thing left in your fridge. Maybe you'll lose weight over the week: you'll arrive at the door to greet him on the fourth and final day looking waifish, ethereal, as if struck by lightning. Yet somehow impeccably dressed.

You want to be done with this so badly it hurts the bottoms of your feet, keeps your body awake, and promises to be better tomorrow. Then again, it'll say anything to get you to leave.

i. Exposition
The biggest relationship curse of them all is the ceaseless temptation to compare to others. You subject yourself to an endless Instagram parade, throwing clumpfuls of grass from the sidelines, simultaneously pissed and envious that—after only two months, wow! They are just THAT CONFIDENT!—so and so are already living together, so and so just got married and posted the photos everyone liked, and oh, didn't it make them feel so good inside?

You don't feel good. You're nauseous. You notice your body's newfound suspicion that any dip in the normal course of things—too many tears, a stomach clench upon waking—could mean you are pregnant. Convinced, it is, of what it thinks it wants. What it is built to do.

You wonder, if you only knew what your soul was built to do, maybe your brain would step out of the icebox where it has wedged itself, terrified, and rejoin the splattery mess of your heart? Your heart, needy as ever, and a perfect mirror of your larger self. A well-meaning healer might take this moment to say you are a "heart-centric person." But if your heart is front, and that means center, and life is a dartboard from which there is no escape—

Bullseye. On it, written in a child's scrawl: *Pain.*

Beneath it, a single Post-it note containing the words he said before he left to take space, which reminded you of something you'd heard before, not from him, but always to you—

"It used to be so easy."

And it made you want to smack him upside the head with the truth you've known since you were a child: while everyone else gets to observe the world, you—whether you like it or not— are always in costume, feeling everyone else's emotions. Your hands built the backdrop, and you could no sooner extricate yourself from the fabric of things than say, in that moment,

"NOT EVERYTHING IS EASY!"

"I LOVE YOU! THAT IS WHAT MATTERS!"

Instead, you cough up some garbled version of the truth as you wait for your throat to sink to the pit of your stomach, brain crawling into its icy cage, poised to wait out the winter. And wonder.

Can we ever trace the rupture back to one moment in time? When the joints lose lubrication, and everything . . . stops?

When you read books about Buddhism, or pick up the phone and hear a certain voice, you are almost able to grasp that this is a *good* thing. Something you never would have asked for, but desperately need: space to remember who you are.

Because he told you what he needed, and did so in his grown-up words, you are finally able to ask yourself: what do I need?

The very question, however, is littered with memories: a standing-room-only crowd of the ghosts who asked for "space" and then untethered completely. They separated from the earth, from the fertile soil of your body, 'til there was nothing left but a speck in the distance—seen through a fish-eye—and the endless, boring, ferocious male narrative: "I need to go discover myself. Tell the world I love her."

Tell her yourself, you selfish asshole.

And you know, you *know* this man—the one you know you want, the one not quite in front of you, but oh, isn't that the glass he drank from yesterday? Wasn't he *just here?*—did not ask to be crowded by the ghosts of boyfriends past. He did not, in speaking his need, invite in the spirit of every man who kicked you in the place where they knew you'd hurt most: your body, your earth. A place none of you own, but you tend, and you live. They kicked you in your borrowed time. And still, even after all these years, you feel used.

Your body, still carrying the shadow of their DNA, kept you up last night; reminded you, in the ache only blood can remember, of what it felt like to be lonely with another human inside of you. To have someone ignore you even as they took shelter in your caves, spiteful at the fire that spits from the bark it needs to survive. To plow your soil while wearing headphones.

How could they, how COULD they, not feel what they unearthed?

You walk your bare feet over the planks of your apartment, which you've swept three times since he left. It's nine in the morning on the first day of your "break," and you wish you had something more original to say than the fact your heart—it's breaking too. Just like it always was. You just didn't notice it before.

II. ACT TWO

Successful attempts performing "normal human behavior": 36.

You're off the kitchen floor, but just barely. You meet up with a friend, who talks about breaking up with his girlfriend because their paths didn't align. Just a little while ago, you told your boyfriend—or do you call him your partner? Do you remember the names you used to call one another during those early days, when your legs always touched, and you still felt immune?—that even though the two of you were clearly in the muck, at least your values aligned. At least. At most, you were once invincible.

"She's just … in outer space," your friend says. "I don't need that."

You ask what he means.

"She's absorbed in herself, and these ideas of what is taking her higher. She thinks she's better than me. But like I said—she's way, way out there."

You wonder, like a child who looks at the stars and sees electrified outlines of lions and queens, what it feels like to be all the way out there. If you could draw a picture, it would be of a young girl's eyeballs; but instead of the color blue, there would be water inside of her irises. You wonder:

1. If when we all have babies, we will stop being so obsessed with our existential crises.
2. If you are actually ahead of the curve by caring about another person more than you care about yourself.
3. Why self-help books tell you this is wrong, but society never gave you the tools to be anything other than what self-help books call "codependent."
4. Is being obsessed with your partner's thoughts and emotions actually a clever way of being obsessed with yourself?
5. You wish you could be obsessed with anything other than him.
6. Maybe Jiu Jitsu. Or knitting. Except,
7. You're a tiny bit afraid of needles.
8. How is it that anyone knows how to make a relationship work?
9. It is an almost impossible task to balance between two people, two points, when all your memories and furniture are stored on one side.

A BRIEF INTERLUDE

The Amazon Rainforest: 2,700,000 square miles, 9 nations, 390 billion individual trees divided into 16,000 species.

Larger still: your need for validation.

(Act out)

ii. Rising Action

Ihatethatthisishappening. Imissyou; Imissyou; Imissyou. Whatareyouthinkingabout? Haveyoueventhoughtabout meonetime? I'msurethisisgreatforyou, andyouusewordslike renewalandactuallymeanit, whenthisishellforme. Itishell, and Ican'teventellyoubecausewe'renotallowedtospeak, orrather

youaskedforthat, andIdon'tunderstandhowyoucangofrom
lookingintomyeyesandseeingthefuturetonotwantingtotalk
tomeatall, andIknowit'sgoodforusboth, andIknowyou're
actuallybehavinginahealthyway, butIdon'tevenwanttogotothe
grocerystorebecauseImightsee, youandyou'reonyourwayto
seesomeoneelse, andmyhairprobablywon'tevenlookgood,
likeitdoesrightnow, butthenagain, you'renotheretoseeit, sodoes
itevenmatter? Does it matter?

iii. Climax
DOES ANY OF THIS EVEN FUCKING MATTER??

Intermission

If this space doesn't remind him (you) of who you truly are,
of all your depth and light and the Christmas wreath of colors
he (you) fell in love with in the first place, and to miss you in
his (your) core, then it isn't meant to be.

Who are you actually writing this for?

III. ACT THREE

Successful attempts at accepting all things as "normal human
behavior": 312.

Suddenly, out of the pain, a gentleness emerges: with no warning, fanfare, or promise of getting easier. It echoes your early
twenties; the loneliness you navigated, and the lovers you left
because they tried to break you, just to finally be ready for the
one who wants to hold all of you. Who doesn't try to fix you
because you are not a broken thing. Suddenly, there emerges
a hand who buys pink zinnias, slows down when looking at
strangers, and a voice who says things like:

"I wouldn't have chosen this, but . . ."

"This is the only way, and . . ."

"I remember the first time I felt this way. Maybe . . ."

"This has nothing to do with him at all, and everything to do with . . ."

"What is it in me that feels so broken, so terrified, so certain I'm the only one who feels the world like this?"

You remember your Stages of Alone. What have you learned about your darkness since then? You schedule an emergency therapy session, spend $60 on organic produce, and shave your legs in the shallow, cool water left at the bottom of the tub. You listen to Joni Mitchell, pay your dental bill on time, and drink French wine that tastes like jam. You don't write in your journal, because it feels like a suckfest, so you let your legs do the speaking. You dance. You put on gloves and hit bags full of sand while '80s music plays in the background. You go to the sea as the sun goes down, dip your body beneath the cool waves, and fill a small bottle with salt water so you can have a witchy ritual. You hear it's the first of several super moons. You hear that can do a number on one's ability to regulate her emotions.

You're the same and you are different from the last time you felt this alone.

You hear from your parents, cousins, coworkers, and friends. You hear the sound of cars passing by your house at night. You see yourself driving and believe you might be the first person ever to understand the appeal of soft rock. You can't help it. You just hear things so clearly.

And today, halfway, you start to understand why.

iv. Falling Action

No one could have done it for you, even you. Could have replaced the jaw-eating sadness of *youusedtowanttodothose thingswithme.*
With a small hand who waves up from the water, and quietly says: *Imissyou.*
I miss you, and maybe this is how you love me right now.

Because you know he loves you, misses you too, and can probably reach an imagined hand across the divide—if not the rest of his body, not yet—and trace the tip of his index finger across your forehead. Down the slope of your nose, over the pillow of your mouth, to rest in the strand of hair he tucks and untucks from your ear. Here with your friends, your fear, and your sadness—all of them needing your attention— you realize how badly they wanted to be with you, and they missed you when you dove into your partnership.

They miss you just as much as you long to be with him. And you will. Just as soon as there's room for both of you to breathe.

You settle on a quick phone call to discuss the location of your coming back together; you listen to the comfort of his voice through the tears that streak over the screen of your phone.

"I'm still in a relationship with you during this time," he says. "I'm still loving you during this time."

Silence creeps through the space between, still uncertain of itself, still heavy in its heels.

"You there?" he asks.

Yes, you reply.

"Good. Me too.

"We're both still here."

IV. ACT FOUR

Four days? Seriously, that's it?

It's entirely possible he may never realize, nor understand, what a big deal this has been for you. It's entirely possible he, along with everyone else, may never understand you at all. You had to wrestle with your demons in order to show up again; you had to wait four days, only four days, for the moon to do its thing. You wrap yourself inside of the thought, let it creep over your brain; and for once, don't feel strangled by it.

Wrap it up, quickly! Doesn't it seem like it's wrapping up quickly?

You notice, exponentially humbled by your human experience, how often you desire a clean ending: for life to tie itself into silky bows at the end of each act, the way it does in movies, or in your imaginary narrative about the Facebook posts of former lovers. All to form a perfect story in your mind, holding hands like paper dolls, sliced from the larger projection of who you think you want to be.

Instead, life really is like a dream. No beginning or ending, no getting back into the unconscious plot after your leg jerks awake and you might have to pee. No understanding why that monster was there. There is only this moment now, you walking to the window on the morning of the fourth day, opening it slowly, and letting sleep fall from your body—awake, but still tentative. Partially here. Partially gone. You remember the story you told him, of the birth of fairies, and how the mother had probably looked into her child's eyes without knowing his heart was breaking; but remembered, perhaps in her throat, that she was once a baby as well. There are things she gave up for the possibility of magic, sometimes with her consent. Sometimes without.

You close your eyes and imagine once again the version of yourself who died in the dream. She's the same one who looked over her shoulder as a child, wandered farther and farther away from her mother, and waited for her face to turn—to let her know:

It's okay! Keep going! This distance will not make you lose me.

And up until now, that child has been looking. Waiting for security which will never come.

So she let you spear her, straight down the line, for a future you are only just beginning to claim: where taking space from your lover means taking UP space, where outer space is INNER space, and every moment you spend walking forward—without validation—is a reclamation of your damp, rich, inner earth. You reject the kind of man who ravages the soil, every single time they suggest that—as women—it is our job to care about everyone but ourselves. Who keep us gridlocked in fear of abandonment so we may never touch upon our truest power, or the places that cannot be stolen: the parts that, upon spearing, grow stronger. Bloom.

It is only in the space created by four days of silence where you realize: the man you love is not that kind of man. He wants to tend you, to stand in awe of you, all the mountains and valleys and scraggly grass—but only if you're willing to do the same. To claim your own landscape, and revel in the burn scars you're meant to make beautiful. To realize you have all you need; sitting under the same tree you used to draw pictures of, and suddenly—powerfully—not waiting for anyone else to arrive.

v. Dénouement
Four days equals four months equals four minutes
And the longest you've ever gone
Feeling as good as you do right now
With only yourself to blame.

EPILOGUE: RAPPROCHEMENT

You learn, utterly humiliated, that you aren't actually in your Saturn Return. Yours is coming a bit later than most: just like the first time you bled through your pants, and the rest of the school had already gotten over the intrigue. So you can't blame Saturn for all your problems, but you can use its mythos to ask for what you really need: to respect another person's time, and for yours to be respected in return. For someone to make use of your energy without using it up, and to leave it better. Like they would your body. Like they could the earth.

You wait for your boyfriend to arrive on the evening of the fourth day, yellow dress hanging off your shoulders like a ceremony. Your bones are stronger than they were before. Your flesh is bigger. Softer. Like the gaze you keep as you look over your shoulder—no longer searching for a face to say it's safe to go; but instead, for the smile that envelops you, warmly, as you finally make your way back.

You didn't believe anyone could come back. And he does. And the pain of waiting was worth it to face yourself, to move things forward, to a place where a conversation can happen: unguarded. Alone, together.

> Would you believe me if I told you?
> There is electricity in the place
> where you turn your soft body, waiting,
> and let it be seen?

You walk to the window just in time to see him getting out of his car, door closing with a click behind him, an audible marker of the phase now ready to end. He catches your eye: you both smile, and you can sense the path unfolding, even if you can't see it. You like where it's going.

According to Rupi Kaur, how he leaves tells you everything. That may be true. But the world is held by how you both return; and return you do. Return you will.

Just like Saturn does. In his own time.

Benedict Uterus

We didn't start out this way, her and me. I hear she began forming four weeks after I was conceived, which sounds ridiculous, but I'm reluctant to Google it, just in case my computer finally short-circuits into a copy of *Taking Charge of Your Fertility.* Because apparently I have transformed into a basic, almost-thirty-year-old mushball who tears up when she sees a baby on the street, like literally tears up at this stranger's baby who isn't even super cute but represents some phenomenal Victory in a way I can't describe. It's just a feeling that, apparently, began forming at four weeks old. I don't remember. But I know we didn't start out this way.

About fourteen years in, she started shedding, and we began cultivating a Herculean tolerance for embarrassment. The peak: summer theater camp. The room was sweaty and smelled of developing pubes. The first day I got my period, I bled through brand-new white jeans and attempted to hide the whole thing by doing a little half-perch on a folding table . . . only to have it collapse beneath me in a pile of metal and shame. My social status never recovered. But my uterus and I? We were good. I discovered the magical currency of Tampax and let the fingers of plasticky cotton rattle around in my backpack like the percussion of womanhood; proof my body was working, that I mattered enough to be able to make life—a thought that barely occurred until years later, standing in the parking lot of Amoeba Records, telling my best friend I'd had sex for the first time.

"At least . . . I think I did. He was definitely . . . *in*. But only for a minute before . . . and what if the condom didn't work? What if one GOT OUT??" Despite living in California, we were still the generation of health classes taught to Fear the Sperm; to believe one could get pregnant anytime, with the likelihood doubled if you were about to attend the college of your dreams. My mother, being equal parts neurotic and psychic, showed up to my workplace that week and slapped a piece of paper onto the counter. "Here," she hissed. "I made you an appointment at Planned Parenthood."

Now convinced sperm were the enemy, and also that my *molecules* had shifted as a result of having a penis almost all the way inside of me, I told her everything. "I don't KNOW if we actually did it. It didn't really . . . work."

And my mother laughed, and we cry-hugged, and I got myself birth-controlled up for the rest of my teens and early twenties. The anxiety attacks began about two years in—but at least I wasn't a teen mom. And then I moved to Bali, ran out of birth control, and for the first time in years, my uterus spoke up. *Hello, stranger! We are now past the age where it is socially inappropriate to get pregnant. Giddy up!*

I knew things were going to change—but they wouldn't take me over the falls yet. We hadn't met the right man quite yet.

At twenty-five, we were complacent, if not a little confused. I had just completed the date-a-million-assholes rite of passage defining the early twenties and was spit out sadder, wiser, but relatively intact. Driving eighty miles per hour to purchase Plan B because I'd rather combust into flames than bear the child of a cold-hearted Instagram model? Not the stuff of dreams. But he smelled so *good.* I remember another gem—let's call him Bucket Hat—mansplaining that *of course* I found men with dark skin attractive because our babies would have the best chance of survival (my skin being the color of an inside-out grape). Mind you, this is the same dude who waited until he was thrusting inside of me to tell me he didn't think we should see each other anymore. But my uterus? Again, she loved his smell. I didn't get her logic, and she didn't see why I needed it—but at our core, we had each other, unfolding in a series of silken epiphanies; like the kind of lover we hadn't yet had but dreamed of.

And then I turned twenty-six. I began asking more questions and watched as three of my friends became doulas, using words like *dilated* and *cervical mucus* like common vernacular. They pulled from the vocabulary we shared somewhere deep in our marrow but had forgotten amidst a chorus that repeatedly tells us our bodies are a) shameful, b) disgusting, c) mysterious, d) and not even that important to begin with. So I soaked up their knowledge like a maxi pad and awakened to my own cycles with a fervor I normally reserve for musical theater, or stalking ex-boyfriends. On the morning of my twenty-seventh birthday, I sat on the lip of a stone wall in Ireland, knowing I had changed.

"I just feel like I need to *create* something, you know? But it's okay. I'm making a bunch of lasagna."

"Oh honey," an older friend laughed. "That's great. But at some point, the lasagna just won't be enough."

Fast forward one month. A wondrous man with briny-blue eyes enters my life like a tidal wave . . . and I welcome the water. Like a person, like a body-desert, who is unmistakably ready to become the wetlands, to make life.

So this man and I poured into one another, and, suddenly, from the perspective of one who is getting regularly, exquisitely laid by the man of her dreams, the thought of having a baby felt . . . different. I began charting my fertility like a scientist with a high-stakes mission; no matter how long

I spent ensuring I did NOT get pregnant, there was a part of me who kinda, sorta, hoped I *did*. And it terrified me.

This lady, meanwhile, LOVED the attention. It was all I could do not to build her a shrine on the mantle—of the home I share with a man who, mind you, calls it my "moon time" and has *literally* gotten on his knees to thank me for being a "bearer of life." Who sat with me in therapy as we discussed the now customary, crippling PMS fueling our household. Who attempted, genuinely, to understand as I tearfully described how the process of bleeding—once a welcome indicator of my freedom—now felt like a harbinger of grief, of unrealized life. By the time I hit twenty-nine, it was clear I no longer related to my uterus alone. Whether in combat or cahoots, it had always been the two of us; now, there was the addition of a clock. And we were three.

And, of course, I tried talking about it with my woke, oh-so-respectful beloved. The fact he'd fallen in love with a woman who was now approximately 50 percent human being, 50 percent baby-shower-bingo was beside the point: we were committed, it was kosher to talk about the future. "Do you want that? A family, with me?"

"I . . . yes," he answered, honestly. "I see it. But I have . . . doubts."

And with his one comment, I felt my uterus go dark. I suddenly recalled the ex-lover who cheated but held me by the pelvis, saying "I'm going to put a baby in you" like he was picking out real estate. I recalled my years as a waitress, watching groups of women huddled over mango margaritas; voices low as they plotted FBI-level strategy for how to *catch, keep,* and *maintain* that one guy who won't text back but would probably make a great dad. I heard fear shake their voices and eventually those of my friends as they discussed freezing their eggs. And who can blame them? We are the women coming-of-age in a world claiming to give us freedom, but still makes the choice for us; who pay with our freaking ORGANS for the fact the people who painted our buildings and made our mascara do not give a shit about our hormones. They never did. And so many men are cowering in the corner, stuck between a rock and toxic masculinity; the rock being the part who remembers what it is to offer a foundation for the feminine to float, unmoored, through the abstract wisdom living in our bodies. But instead, women are kicking ourselves for drinking hot beverages out of plastic cups, fearing the casual conveniences that may have decided our lives, or the lives we want to create. And what about the casual decisions, the sex-in-restaurant-bathrooms, leading to those lives in the first place? Was I one of those accidents? What does it even mean to be free?

My parents weren't married when they had me. This has been, alternatingly, a huge and negligible detail throughout my life. From the place of one who is snowballing, however, the question of whether I was wanted, whether *they* wanted each other, was everything. I turned to my mother one day, probably on Day 2 of my period, and asked the question I was always afraid of. Her eyes got big and her body softened, as though it remembered what it felt like to feed me. "YOU," she whispered, "were ALWAYS wanted. I prayed for you."

My uterus stirred, emerging from her fear-cave. The next day, I turned to my dad—who apparently went camping for a week when he found out my mom was pregnant. He was thirty-seven.

"Did Mom force you to become my father and then drive you nuts by talking about marriage until you eventually broke down and threw Grandma's ring at her on the lawn?"

"Are you kidding? NO." His expression said everything. "Let's just say this. No one can make me do anything I don't want to do."

And the Freudian perfection is not lost on me that I have chosen a partner who ALSO will not be pressured into

A-Ny-Thing. And it makes me trust him *more.* If we choose to be parents, it will be that: a choice. Not the result of coercion ("YOUR HONOR") or molding, Gumby-style, into whatever I think he wants me to be. My grasping for some sort of rug beneath my feet, hoping he can offer the right words RIGHT NOW to make me feel less out-of-control, is just a fancy form of flailing. Booby-trapping for signs of danger ("Do you like the name Jack? What do you mean, kind of? Does that mean you don't want a family? DO YOU EVEN LIKE ME AT ALL?") is simply a clever way of robbing myself of the present moment. And truth be told, the present moment is scary; as a planet, we are in uncharted waters. At times, I consider the incessant, make-a-baby throb of my organs to be similar to the way my cat scratches at the ground after taking a dump in her litter box. The kitchen could be going up in flames, and still she would scratch; because at some point instinct takes over, and it is what she knows to do.

My uterus too. We are just doing what we know to do — or what we didn't even know we knew, but have somehow come into, like a pile of riches. Or responsibility. Today, when my boyfriend asks me about any of it, my head no longer spins 360 degrees on its axis; I simply stop my sunflower-planting, or lasagna-baking, or compulsive needlepointing and answer that making life no longer feels negotiable. And he listens. He'll never be trapped by her needs.

I, however, might always be. And that's okay.

And maybe the only feeling of safety I will ever find in this fundamentally unsafe world must come from the same place that spat me into it: She. Not my enemy. Part of my body. As flesh-and-blood as the human who may one day come from her, asking only for what she is also prepared to give me: everything.

Call Your Mother

Would you believe me if I said the reason I'm late is because
I was clearing the matrilineal line of my family?

How 'bout if I said: the reason I can't stop crying is because a
mountain of matriarchs told me they wanted to go for a swim?

The thing is I am a daughter, and my mother a daughter, and
we are granddaughters of a million versions of moon,
And sometimes they're waxing poetic
'Bout everything they have done wrong.

And I'm here, like a crescent, bending under their backs,
Trying to remember to get back
Up and splash cool water on my face, meet my own gaze in
the mirror and say, "You look good in that shirt!"
But I forget, sometimes,
Not to chew my own tongue as I'm falling asleep,
Praying for something to break,
Preying upon the hell they taught me to make.
Would you forgive me if I told you it's for my great-grandma?

Or for my mother, perhaps, who never told me about the conversations they had
Before she walked in on him cheating,
Or what color socks she wore
When she felt like a rainbow inside.
I want to say I'm not like my mother,
But look at these freckles splashing my cheeks
And honestly say you believe me.
I want to say I won't make her mistakes, but what if in that exact moment
She's already coming to get me, like the shadow that sits in each unanswered call
and the feeling of watching him walk out the door and the what if I'm never, what if I'm never, what if I'm never, ever, EVER enough?

Would you believe me if I told you, then, that I'm doing it for myself?
Making an accidental offering from the side of my hand, writing a song that plays
Clingy and Desperate like pawns on a board
Made of ivory skin,
And the questions she asked
Over coffee one day, "Do you know you're a star? Do you know?"

I ask my unborn daughter what she wants me to do, and she smiles at me from her throne.
Puts down her sandwich of sunrises and expensive falafel and tells me I have to: grow up.

Shit.

She tells me to tell them to give up the ghost. To put down the cross and build the damn church. To show me their hand and then call it a flush and then call off their dogs and then call me a cab and then call me my name, my NAME, the first name of a new line of women who believe in the kindness of men and the worth that makes the measuring stick shudder and break and say "give me a break, you've been here the whole time?" The kind of glorious, generous, un-fuck-withable YES that comes shooting from out of my skull as I say:

I was BORN to make LOVE from this PAIN.

To tell them I'm sorry, but you seem to have forgotten that I am not like you.
I was born on the earth to eat my own fire, then spit droplets of silver that dance in the rain.
I am the daughter of a thousand kisses, and if you crack open my bones, eleven lightning bolts will shoot out and smash their hands together, shake in their rose-colored boots and howl second-hand raps at the moon.
I came from you but I am not yours, I am his, and I am mine, I am MINE, I am mine in the morning and mine in the night when the weight of all you forgot to let go of gets stacked like old bones on a shelf and my face scrunches up with your mouth and your eyes, but my brain, and my PAIN—
This pain, which I claim,
Which I no longer turn from,
Which she can't talk out of me,
And I can't drink out of me,
And they can't twist out of me,
And he can't fuck out of me
But we, we can sing out of me—one, two, three—

'Til it hovers, like a thousand glistening notes, in the space above my chest, and my eyes turned up to the sky and the hollow that finally says *I love you, come inside.*

You see. The moment I decided to finally let them in was the moment I could finally let them go.

She and the quiet desperation of what she wished would have happened

She and the searing void where she couldn't make it stop,

She and the realization that even the best pair of arms that wrap all the way, two times round the Earth, will one day let go and give back to the ground.

Mother. Would you believe me if I told you that everyone leaves? That I'm no longer afraid?

I want you to look at me like an infant does, like the one I once was, and say into my spine: *you were never an accident.*

To crawl out of my veins

And the house in my head

And instead take your place by my side

In my life,

Where you've always been wanted,

Where we've always been free.

PART IV:

Full

Starfucker

VOL. 1: PHANTOM

Now that I am married and incredibly old, at least by Hollywood standards, I spend a lot of time thinking[11] about a time when I was neither. My favorite thing to bring up with strangers (who have not asked) is the era in which I had sex with famous people. It wasn't something I sought out, really, more like something nice that happened, and I felt made me look better. Like an especially good haircut, or going on vacation with someone else's parents.

Living as we do in a world where women are ranked by our ability to apply liquid eyeliner[12] — not to mention having a mother who was once asked out by JFK Jr. (she declined) — when first presented with celebrity attention, a voice rose up from deep within my womb and said: "Hey! Since we're not using this yet, wanna blow a bunch of self-esteem on people who have made a career of seeking validation from other, less attractive humans?" The answer in the moment was an unequivocal yes.

What happened next was decidedly less clear.

---

11. obsessing.
12. I am HORRIBLE at this.

Sometimes I wonder what snagged me in the first place. Perhaps it was unconscious rebellion against the education I received and will pay off approximately $37 at a time; I attended an intense women's college, where my peers were more likely to recite Adrienne Rich while chained to a tree than accept googly eyes from someone *People* magazine once called an emerging hottie. Relationships with men were typically shouldered as inevitable, unnecessary roadblocks on the way to becoming the first female president.

However, in the years after graduation—my long-term, long-distance relationship finally kaput—I stood at a crossroads: armed with a degree telling me I didn't need the approval of men, I made a beeline for the least available, most self-absorbed man in the room, and hung my hopes (and probably my bra) upon him. Take that, feminism!

At least one of these men was a sociopath. Two happened to be celebrities, which, in case you were wondering, does not make them more emotionally intelligent or important than the average bear. For one hot moment; however, they made ME feel more important—because why cultivate something from deep within when you can get it from someone who doesn't fly coach and probably has a stalker?

To be clear: I'm not a stalker. I've seen plenty on TV, and while I salute those ladies for maintaining impeccable lip gloss whilst lurking outside their married lover's house with a kitchen knife, I would sooner combust than "accidentally" run into someone whom I've pinpointed via Instagram. Don't get me wrong—I know stalking is serious. And still, every time I found myself waiting for texts from shiny men (my twenty-something equivalent of an Olympic sport[13]), it would become clear the sheen of our encounter had worn off. For them, the magic had been replaced with something like

---

13. GOLD MEDALIST

fear—and later, conviction—that the only reason I might want to reach out is because I needed something. And the more they feared it, the more I *did* need something; however, that alone didn't mean texting "hello" was actually a diversion before handing over my firstborn and asking them to sign it.[14]

I learned slowly, not quickly, that doubt is contagious. Between bouts of internal gymnastics and waiting for text responses that wouldn't come, this era of my life saw me crawl through the wreckage of what used to feel like self-esteem, turning over occasional pieces of rubble like old, mysterious stones and finding nothing. At one point, I was desperate enough to write a text that began with "Sir, I am not trying to . . ."| and ended with ". . . harvest your DNA and sell it on eBay," which landed about as well as any text about sperm ever does.

Like I said, I'm not a stalker. But I've seen a lot of movies, I know how this shit works. What they never show you onscreen, though, is exactly how many breaths—or cold cups of tea—it takes to wait for someone to write *haha, your*[15] *funny,* when only weeks before you had breathed the same rich air, had held the same magic between your faces, and still believed it could grow.

So, I waited for texts and I would have done anything. Anything to refuse the creeping belief that these men might want to ignore me, and their behavior might suggest something about me, rather than them.

The first time I met Phantom, I was still one of the unknowns. It was a college music festival; he was packing his guitars, and I had short, spiked hair I'd doused in blue glitter. He was cute

---

14. Hire me, *Lifetime.*
15. Don't date someone who doesn't know the difference between "your" and "you're," unless they are doing it ironically, and even then, don't do it. You're welcome.

and wore suspenders. What could go wrong? After watching him play, I remember feeling a whoosh of familiarity course through my body—a bone-deep knowing, a longing to just place my forehead near his to feel the contents of his mind slosh around. While I probably looked like I was in the Ice Capades, I felt like a million bucks and did not hesitate to invite him to the *totallychill* party happening that night at my house, which was, of course, a co-op full of dirty hippie boys and warm local beer. But he didn't need to know that yet.

"I'll try," he replied, and I pranced away, genuinely hoping he'd be there mainly so I could prove to my friends I'd been weird enough to approach him, to say a few witty things, and just be near his forehead. The feeling of familiarity was strong enough I knew not to question it. But he never came to the party, and I forgot he existed.

Flash forward one year: another music festival, this time in Oregon, where a three-hundred-day winter had paved way for the kind of shit-eating grin that says "I'm wearing a flower crown, now what?" I had just moved to Portland, was nannying two small children during the day, and had cut ties for the final time with my revolving-door boyfriend, who had recently been arrested for buying crack at a gas station. The bar was low. My spirits, however, were high.

The early mornings of toddler-breakfasts and late-night solo bike rides had rained onto seedlings of self-worth and, by the time I walked into the festival, I was ready. For the first time since my heart had been shattered, I felt curious about its capacity. So it really came less as surprise and more like obvious magic when a familiar cowboy hat bobbed toward me from across a field—dark, rascally eyes locking onto mine— and I knew who it had to be.

"*You*," Phantom practically snarled, the corners of his playful mouth tugging up into a grin. It was a different year, a different state, but the feeling was the same. "Do you have any idea how much I wanted to go to the party at your house? I had a girlfriend, though.

"I don't anymore," he added, eyes glinting.

"That's cool," I slid back to him. The electricity between us could have fried a barn. And thus began a dance from within, no mistaking: this is all yours.

Until the next day, when it watered down to 50 percent ours, 50 percent what other people might think. That's the thing about fucking around with famous people: even the most well-assured, confident woman[16] is subject to the parasitic dumpster fire of adoring friends and chorus of "OMG! Are you *serious*?" that comes in the aftermath. At that point in my life, I had army-crawled my way toward the capacity for real romance, but I was by no means confident, nor assured. And like high-fructose corn syrup, the approval and envy following my first night with Phantom filled some empty space inside and left me hungrier than before. And for someone like me, who had only recently discovered what it felt like to look in the mirror and like what I saw, the edge between "feeling wanted" and "feeling whole" wasn't just blurry. It was nonexistent.

So, I fell into it every single time someone asked me what had happened. Memories of the night would bat around in my brain like fireflies: *don't go anywhere,* he had told me, face inches away from mine. He had just finished signing my back with a Sharpie,[17] which my friend Reuben photographed with the small digital camera I kept around my wrist. *Don't worry,* I replied, and watched the fire spit. He returned about an hour later, wild curls freshly tucked beneath his hat, the honey-sweet smell of summer and cider wafting off his tanned skin. He came back, and he brought everything. I remember the warmth between our palms as he took my hand, dancing me through

16. Beyoncé.
17. I give myself an F minus for not recognizing this GIGANTIC RED FLAG.

the pre-dawn pines—both of us giddy, stunned at the inexplicable ease in our overlap—stopping only to press his entire body against mine, perching my hips onto a low fence while my stomach did flips and fell out of my toes, his hands gripping my shoulders in firm, determined longing and his mouth kissing my lips with hunger and freedom. Phantom's kisses were like his music: far-reaching, complicated, and eternal. More alive than the others. He invited me to spend the night, but I chose to run into the sunrise and back to my camp—surprising myself with the certainty I felt at knowing I'd see him again. *We have time.* This was mine, wasn't it? Who was I to NOT march right up to him the next day, throw my hands around his neck, and kiss him the way he had kissed me just hours before?

But I didn't. And I wouldn't. Because in the process of telling my friends what had happened, making it more palatable for them, I lost a piece of it myself. And it wasn't until the next time we met up I realized what a difference that piece made.

⌇

A note: I think I missed the day of junior high where everyone explains you have to play it, like, totally cool around people you have crushes on, otherwise, they will run away for the rest of time. Becoming a twenty-something in the dating world was one long extension of that lesson, only, instead of liking someone, the person in question has recently had their genitalia in your mouth. And yet, we are supposed to pretend we don't know them the next day at brunch. ("Oh, this stain on my shirt? It's nothing, really, just the dried semen of the man sitting across from us, who I'm supposed to ignore so he knows I really like him. Anyone want to share the omelet?" BARF.)

Being with a famous person is like that only worse because at any given moment there are forty crop-topped women slinking around and part of the celebrity image (and therefore your agreement) is to allow him to seem single enough for the crop-tops to promote him on Instagram. Many times, the appeal is in other people thinking they have a chance, and, when I'm really being my truest self,[18] there's no room whatsoever for guesswork. After all, I cut my teeth as the daughter of a musician; I had met enough groupies to sink a ship by the time I was twelve, and, by twenty, I had learned the only way to fully shake a fan girl is to get your man to shout your name — *Beetlejuice* style — three times from the stage. Jenna-Jenna-Jenna. Or alternatively, to patrol the scene like armed security. Over the years, however, my personal brand evolved into more of a golden retriever than a pit bull; when I am in love with someone, they *know*. They know because I bound up to them like they've just gotten home from work and lick their face and wag my tail and give absolutely zero shits if it makes me uncool.

But that time, with Phantom onstage for the final day of the festival, a new form of resistance crept into my blood; one that cautioned, *don't show too much, don't expect too much, don't believe, don't.* So I didn't. I watched him play, and I walked away.

It took two months, approximately thirty passes through his album, several text messages, and one perfectly located family reunion for us to end up in the same state again. At which point, we:

a) Met up at a dive bar after it took him four hours to get back to me (so sweet)
b) Took shots of Fireball out of plastic cups (awww)
c) Snuck out the side to talk to some girl he'd recently boned (swoon)
d) Drove to the AirBnB where my family was sleeping (stop, I'm blushing!)

---

18. About seven years old, wearing glittery high-tops and a Talking Heads sweatshirt, watching *Labyrinth*.

e) Had a sloppy make-out session in front of the gate (are we married yet?)

f) Returned to his van to have quick, unemotional sex on the scummy mattress (THEY WILL WRITE SONNETS ABOUT US ONE DAY.)

Afterward, as I stepped out of the car with liquid still dripping down my leg, I waited as he fumbled around a cardboard box. "Here," he muttered, handing me a T-shirt from his tour merch. "It's a little weird," he added, sheepishly. *Yes, I thought.* But still, I knew—like his smell—I would wear it the whole next day.

And even though I had orchestrated the whole thing, had drunk the Kool-Aid and played it cool, the silence that followed felt thick and cottony. I was devastated before, and now my vagina was too. The story I told my friends was the sex with Phantom had been "fantastic," when what had *actually* been fantastic was the synchronicity that hummed beneath our unspoken moments, no matter the level of fuck-all his actions actually communicated.

"I'm just not in a space to give myself lovingly to anyone right now," he had said, right before shoving his hand—super lovingly, I might add—up my shirt. Still, I held onto those ribbons of fate like parachute strings. *What about the fact that we adore the same bizarre things? What about the stories that haunt our bones, which no one gets, but we do? What about the silent moments of recognition? If that's not love, what is?*

Sigh. I'll say it again: I'm not a stalker. But the next time I went to one of Phantom's gigs, after the night in his van,[19] I showed up in my favorite high-waisted jeans, expertly playing the part of Girl Who Watches and Knows What Every Song is About, when in truth, I didn't. And I didn't know him. Or at least, not the full-spectrum man who existed outside of what I

---

19. Or as he called it, the "vansion." You may identify this as another red flag. You are correct.

needed him to be: a spark in the dark matter of a young woman in search of herself. An avatar representing the concept, not reality, of soul-bound love. A backward kick into my own teeth or ANYTHING to get me to work up the courage and admit: *I'm an artist too! Just like you only without a bunch of people watching. Just try and stop me. Try!*

When I finally approached him, he clutched his heart and pretended to fall backward. After all, it's the ones who haven't fallen who can pretend to. I could have said many things.

"The last time we saw each other, you were inside of me. It's super weird we aren't talking about that."

"I think I might love you, which doesn't make any sense, but it's true."

"Will you take a photo with me to post on the internet so I feel less insane and alone?"

But instead, I said nothing.

He began chain-smoking and introduced me to his new singing partner, whose words said, "nice to meet you" but whose body said, "get lost before I stab you with a nail file." I gave him a sloppy kiss on the cheek and pulled away into the night, with words that said "great to see you" but with a body that crumpled in on itself like a broken balloon.

~

There's a snapshot in my head, of the second-to-last time I saw Phantom. Summer heat pulsed off the forest floor where we sat, both staring outward in what could have been perceived as quiet confidence but was actually unbearable awkwardness.

We perched on the edge of a fallen tree, my feet planted firmly beneath me, and his toes tapped down into the soft dirt below, like a person who could get up and run at any moment.

My gaze was turned inward, searching for clues; if I found something to unlock him, it would surely set me free as well. Right? I had just gifted him with my ~~visibly bleeding heart~~ favorite childhood mug, which featured the solitary image of the Phantom of the Opera mask floating over black glaze like a sad UFO. We both loved that musical as kids, and I had never met any other human who shared an affinity for the same creepy, random shit I did. Gifting him with a talisman of childhood felt less like desperation, and more like genuine overflow. His gaze upon those parts of myself, and sharing them, made me feel seen in a way I hadn't, remembered for something primordial that I couldn't yet name, but wanted to be closer to. I mistook it for true understanding.

He turned the mug over in his hands, smiling with the corners of his eyes, but unable to hide a nervous twitch in his lip.

"Are you sure?" he asked, turning his gaze up and forward, back to the new, independent landscape he had chosen without telling me. It was the middle of August, and toward the end of whatever "thing" I thought we were doing. I imagine that for him, it was probably equal parts soul-recognition, terror, and apathy; but for me, for the time being, our connection was still a remnant of the truest electricity I'd ever known. I mean, he was BIG. Like the cosmos in a cowboy hat. Standing up on a stage, sweat pouring from the tips of his hair and into the grooves in his guitar, he had a knack for letting whatever true thing passed through his heart pulse out of his hands and into the open, upturned palms of anyone lucky enough to be there. Watching him, I was met with the undeniable feeling of watching some version of *myself* be completely at ease in front of a bunch of unknown humans—who, by the end, all felt like they'd been together since birth. I didn't want to lose it, ever.

So I sat still, tried to close my hands around it, and faded.

Six months later, I saw Phantom for the last time. A string of northern California wineries whipped by in the golden hour, a fat harvest moon rising over glinting hills. "You act like he's doing you a colossal favor by acknowledging you exist," my friend Alycia sighed as we drove to the venue. *Yeah, but he gave us VIP! That should count for something, right?* "No, Jenna. You have licked this man's earlobe. The least he can do is give you a couple free fucking beer tickets."

But who owes anyone anything? Who decides what we get to expect from those we love, who sometimes love us back, and who remind us of the parts we've forgotten—or perhaps haven't discovered yet? After the show, and the VIP, and the unspoken VIP where we all headed to the band's hotel room—drinking whiskey from the bottle, laughing at nothing and everything—I finally began the long walk back to Alycia's car. I thought about how genuinely happy Phantom had seemed to see me. And as soon as my hand made contact with the car door, I knew with a sinking stomach—the same place that had held butterflies—it was the last time. My last chance to go full golden retriever. So in a moment of 1980s rom-com delusional ecstasy, I turned around; galloping back toward the hotel elevator, I batted breathlessly at the "up" button, just waiting for this to be that *moment*, like in the movie, when the girl finally has her moment, when—the doors opened. Ding. Phantom stood there, flanked by two friends holding ice buckets, and managed to creak out a surprised smile.

"Hi," he said, in the same velvety tone that had once told me I was magical. "Did you forget something?"

Had I? Other than the part of myself who came into the world believing I deserved more from lovers than the polite reciprocity one might give a bartender or to a particularly well-trained dog? Somewhere in the course of longing for Phantom and accepting his fame as an excuse for treating me like yet another thirsty fan, I had lost the thread of myself. Standing in front of the elevator, I thought I wanted Phantom to sweep me up in his arms, to choose me. In retrospect, what I *actually* wanted was confirmation I wasn't crazy for feeling our synergy, which seemed to run so fiercely beneath the marrow of time; or at the very least, for wanting someone who had entered my body, heart, and mind to also be willing to pick up the telephone. If asked then, I probably could have predicted the next few years of random communications on my end, with no response on his. For someone who wrote so profoundly about ghosts, the irony wasn't lost: he would ghost me, and I would haunt my own body with the idea of what could be. I'd rattle my chains with my own unwritten songs, unrealized potential, and desire to be known—'til the point when I'd finally free them, howling, and myself in the process. Maybe all I ever felt was the ghost of the past lives we'd danced in before; of all our mutual mentors, moving through my body like wind. Maybe we could have been more. Maybe we already were.

"No," I replied, which felt true at the time. Because when it came down to it, I didn't need anything in order to remember the knowing or the mirrored glint in his eye. I hadn't dismissed the fire between us. Still haven't.

VOL. 2: BISCUIT

To be clear, "not dismissing" did not exempt me from:

a) Fucking other people in cars with similar results
b) Briefly posting a Tinder profile, which resulted in exactly two dates, including one where the person said I "seemed kinda mean"
c) Lying to myself about what I deserved from a romantic relationship. Which did not, for the record, include,
    1) Being cheated on repeatedly, nor
    2) Holding bags / coats / small dogs for other people while they take selfies with my new, exponentially more famous, lover.

In the years that followed my experience with Phantom, I often referred to him as someone I "dated" just to preserve my own ego (also because "karmic-bound-crush culminating in mediocre van sex and a wistful goodbye" is simply too long to say at the grocery store). Even in Southern California, where dating is often reduced to hanging out after yoga and occasionally making out, I wanted more for myself: and the thought I'd wasted years of precious romantic energy on someone I couldn't even count as having *dated* made my armpits feel clammy and weird. So I lied about Phantom and decided to shift my attention to people who actually ate meals with me.

Then came 2016, and the presidential election; and with it, more than a few nights spent sobbing in my bed, donating to Planned Parenthood in $4 increments, and making dystopian playlists on Spotify.[20] In the daytime, I showed up to as many rallies, protests, and other peaceful-yet-pissed-off gatherings as I could. I aligned myself with people who—like myself—were terrified an actual psychopath rapist was going to assume the presidential office and steal our ovaries and trade

20. Taylor Swift, Duran Duran.

them for hair plugs. So we might as well stop playing it small. Right? Right??

The day of the Los Angeles Women's March, I woke up in my best friend's apartment in West Hollywood. The night before, we had shared M&Ms from a Tupperware container and used magic markers to write things like "NO WOMB FOR YOUR OPINION" and "VIVA LA VULVA" on oversized pieces of construction paper.

"I grew out my armpit hair for this." Isabel beamed through a mouthful of green chocolate. "I'm totally writing that on the back of my poster."

In the morning, as we made our way to the center of the city—reusable water bottles slung over our shoulders—something larger-than-life took over my body. Suddenly, I was transported back to summer in Oregon; light streaming from my fingertips, tall grasses kissing my knees. I wore glitter on the hills at college; I grabbed the microphone in our senior musical; I stood atop a volcano at sunrise, screaming my lungs dry and praying no one dared underestimate my power, lest I fry them with my raw creative prowess and intolerance for anything not my highest good. Maybe it was the energy of the hundreds of thousands of diverse women around us, their bellies protruding and hair matted and mouths open and children beaming, gathered and chanting around us in unison and *demanding* change. Maybe it was the fact I'd worn my favorite jean shirt and eaten a protein-rich breakfast. Whatever it was, I was unstoppable, and I knew whomever I happened to encounter next, romantically or otherwise, would be subject to someone other than the whimpering girl who had "dated" Phantom and was "sorry for the inconvenience, sir," and who always yielded at a four-way stop. I was a motherfucking geyser. So it hardly surprised me when that evening at the Surly Goat[21]

---

21. A bar in West Hollywood where one is as likely to win at shuffleboard as to befriend a male stripper. And yes, both happened to me the same night, and no, I did not buy a lottery ticket because I am a fool. A FOOL.

I passed a table dotted with celebrities, and, instead of walking past, "sorry for the inconvenience, sir," I chose to plop into the too-tight booth and join the conversation. Who were they to turn me away? I was woman, hear me roar. I was infinite.

It took about five seconds for Biscuit's eyes to lock onto me. To be fair, I wore a raw silk dress with an asymmetrical hem. And to be extra fair, I wasn't pretending not to recognize him—I genuinely didn't. The other man in the booth starred in a Netflix show I had recently devoured, and my full attention was on how long I would have to make small talk before I could ask for a fun fact about Laura Prepon. After twenty minutes of listening to him speak instead about the re-feminization of US power structures, I slid my attention across to Biscuit. He had been waiting quietly, in that way British people do, inserting one or two clever jabs when the moment necessitated but otherwise maintaining a churning, rainforest silence growing more intriguing by the second. Three beers later, he perched on the side of the booth next to me, his back against the open-grate of the bar periphery, his attention noticeably absent from the few women who had walked by, done a double take, and paused with their faces cut up in the grate-light.

"Can you give me a spoiler alert? What happens next season? Why did you get killed off??"

"It's funny," he would tell me the following month, as we walked to buy condoms from CVS in a neighborhood that wasn't his own. Less likely to be spotted there. "Everyone wants to know what happens next on the show or the deeper meaning behind the plot twist. But it's like, do I ask a bunch of questions when YOU lose your job?"

We would laugh at this, eventually, but we're not there yet. Right now we are still at the bar, and the lights are snapping on because it's 2:00 a.m., and the laws of regular life have yet to reapply. Some girl is talking about a party in the hills, and the celebrities are piling into an Uber. Isabel, who is visibly drunk at this point, splatters into the middle seat; Biscuit rolls down the window, closes his eyes, and pours his very expensive face out the window. A light rain has started, and the asphalt is steaming. The fabric on the seat between us is steaming. And again, that feeling, no mistaking it: this is all yours.

Now, imagine you have a View-Master; the kind we used to have when we were kids, where a series of Technicolor images are displayed in an order making perfect sense from start-to-finish. You realize there have to be certain things miss-ing—like, how did that dog get over there so fast? What about the rest of the fence?—but you keep looking anyway, because the colors are bright, and the rest of the world becomes invis-ible. So in chronological order:

1. WE ARE AT A PARTY IN LAUREL CANYON AND EVERYONE IS DRUNK

I have no idea who owns this house. Someone has just offered me red wine in a glass tumbler, which I take without thinking. The pile of rose-shaped soaps in the bathroom could probably finance my car. I walk outside. My dress has grown sticky from the combination of sweat and drizzle, and even though it's January, I'm not cold. Biscuit and I walk to a wooden bench overlooking a backyard strung with fuzzy lights. Or are the lights clear, and I'm fuzzy? I can no longer feel my head. Someone is attached to a blond girl at the picnic table, their faces hidden behind her curtain of hair. Someone is sliding a hand up her leg. Someone is placing a hand on MY leg. I turn to see Biscuit, staring at me—no, better, *looking* at me—and feel my eyebrows soften. His eyes are tiger eyes, turned inside out by honey-brown stripes and bottomless craving. He leans in and kisses me like they do in the movies. No, better! Like they do in real life. This is real life, only more colorful, right? And this person who shouldn't even speak to me—well, he smells like fresh-cut grass and is running his hands through my hair. When we pull apart, the celestial bodies over the Canyon seem to spin in a chorus of *I told you so.*

2. HER ROOMMATE HAS JUST BOUGHT THAT COUCH AND NOW WE ARE HAVING SEX ON IT

We have taken a car back to Isabel's apartment, and I stop briefly to make tea. Does he take milk? Does he want some noodles? This seems like a really good time to eat noodles, but, no, it is me he wants, and I want him back, and I don't care that he has some hesitation. I'm used to hesitation. There is always hesitation! Someone always has someone they are getting over or someone they want to be getting over, and my brain always thinks it can step in and snot all over the kisses that should feel candid. On this night, though, magnetism cuts through the mud. The streets are teeming with the memory of female feet, pounding the asphalt, saying *NO WAY WILL YOU STOP ME.* My own voice, crackling, demanding the change that begins here: finally, no longer expecting the abuse or the sadness of men to take over the amphitheater of my heart. My glowing, beating, creative heart has opened to this man— this man who the WORLD has validated as having a creative heart! The world wants him—just ask the magazines—and has decided to send the message to open my body as well.

I pull him to the couch, which had been lugged up the stairs only hours earlier by Isabel's new roommate. We leave the curtains open so the air can pour in. He enters me effortlessly, like warm water, and in that moment I know he will never meet my family. But in meeting, in merging, I feel a part of myself wake up after being asleep for a long, long time: *I'm here. Feed me, and I will never leave you. Love me, and I will always feed you.* It is morning by the time we are done, more than morning, it is 8:30 a.m. People are awake and getting breakfast burritos around the corner as he leaves his first, middle, and last name in my phone, along with a message—*you are infinite*. Isabel's roommate rounds the corner in a T-shirt, presumably to pee, and rubs her eyes. It's unclear if she sees me, Biscuit, the couch, or all three. We are no longer separate.

3. THIS IS A SUPER CONVENIENT TIME FOR ME TO VISIT

In the day that follows, I drift in and out of sleep on the couch and do not hesitate to text him. I hesitate 10 percent more the following day and 25 percent more the day after. By the end of the week, nearly all the fairy dust has evaporated from my vision, and I have replaced the memory of Biscuit's tongue in my mouth with the logical assumption I made the entire thing up, was probably mistaken for someone else, and should definitely consider therapy. Then my mother reminds me we are traveling to visit family in Texas and will be flying out from LAX on Friday. Do I want to carpool or meet her there? I give myself zero time to agonize and instead text Biscuit, my hands shaking. *I will be in LA Thursday night. Want to meet up?* He answers within minutes, and my stomach shoots into my eyeballs. Several days later, and seven hours before I am supposed to meet my mom at the airport, I arrive at his door—he answers, shirtless. Are you kidding? They really do that sort of thing? We talk about Shakespeare for three or four minutes before he has me on the floor, my body warm beneath him, my heart warm inside the tunneling gaze of his award-winning attention. We decide we will get Mexican food, and maybe a drink—but later. Later.

4. BUT WHERE IS HIS FURNITURE?

I'll call it a fair assumption that someone who makes approximately five gajillion times more money than I do might also be the kind of someone who has basic things in their home: bed, chair, can opener. I have built my castle of lies on assumptions such as these, about men and the things they will offer me. Biscuit, bless his heart, did not even have a clean towel. Random bottles of supplements designed to promote energy and vitality? Sure. Smattering of mismatched gift mugs, their ceramic sides reading *Late Night with Jimmy Fallon* and *The View*? Definitely. I pour some post-coital water into *Good Morning America* and wait for Biscuit to come out of the bathroom. His bed is an expensive mattress laid on the floor, patchworked by several blankets with "Netflix" printed in the corners. I flip through a pile of Polaroids featuring the glowing smile of several other unusually attractive TV stars, all enjoying a night at the most expensive hotel in Southern California. I look up at Biscuit's beautiful, real-life body that has just emerged in the glow of the overhead bulb and smile. I'd go to the bathroom too, but there is no toilet paper.

5. WE SHOULD PROBABLY MAKE A PLAN TO MEET UP

We've been at this for a month now and why bother making a plan when it is soooo thrilling to check my phone every five or six minutes, wondering if Biscuit has texted me back? Oh, he can meet up tonight? We should get Thai food but need to wait until after he has finished going over lines for an audition? That's okay, I can wait. How much longer? Two hours? No problem, it's only 9:30 p.m. What's that? He wants to see me again tomorrow? Okay, I'll just quit my job and abandon my friends and live on Isabel's couch while I wait for him to give me a fifteen-minute heads up each time he has a free window to bone and listen to the White Album, before waving good-bye as he heads back to a glamorous premiere or photo shoot or gallbladder massage or whatever other bizarre Hollywood shit he does. Who, me? I'll be here, just going with the flow. What can I say? I'm just chill like that.

6. IT'S VALENTINE'S DAY, BUT THAT'S NOT A BIG DEAL

Except it is. It's a big, fucking deal, and I'm tired of going with the flow. I'm tired. I haven't slept in my own bed for days, and now I'm waiting outside of Cofax for Biscuit to bike over and join me for breakfast burritos. Yes, it's Valentine's Day. And sure, once upon a time, I actually had a boy wait in our high school choir room with a sign around his neck that read "Will You Be My Valentine?" and I never thought to question whether I deserved it. But this is obviously better, because Biscuit has several dedicated hashtags, and they're trending! And because Valentine's Day, like all other corporate holidays, was invented by the patriarchy and should therefore be ignored. Which I do, as Biscuit shows up and gives me a dry peck on the cheek, and I offer to pick up the tab on our breakfast. He refuses, because he is a gentleman, and also an actual movie star millionaire; I forget this sometimes because he wears mismatched socks and seems legitimately intimidated by my vagina. But that doesn't make it less true.

We walk to Pan Pacific Park in silence and have just decided to climb a tree when a woman jogs by, does a double take, and then turns back to talk to us. "Hello!" she yells too loudly. "It is a very good person who climbs a tree in a public park. Do you want me to take your picture?" The following week, I am eating breakfast with this woman—her name is Melissa—while I wait for Biscuit to text and determine my fate for the day. Somehow, I have gone from asphalt-stomping feminist in a raw silk dress to fragmented phone girl, bending so far backward in an effort to seem "chill" that I might end up biting my own ass. It's Phantom all over again. Something has to give. I look up with sad dog eyes toward Melissa, who clearly knows about these things, but probably doesn't know Biscuit is famous, and I am a person who fucks famous people—otherwise she would have said something. Right? Because it makes everything different. Right?

"No, I know who he is," she laughs through a bite of scrambled egg. "I just don't give a shit."

7. HE'S OUT OF CONDOMS

I drop Melissa at her apartment and proceed to walk aimlessly through the Container Store, perusing a riveting array of Tupperware. After an hour, my phone buzzes and, again, before I can even climb into the Lyft, I get a prickling sensation and know it will be the last time I see Biscuit. I arrive and, before I've finished my mug of *Conan O' Brien* tap water, his hands cupping my face into a kiss, I know the sex will be bad. But it's not until he is actually hovering over me, panting, asking if I have a condom, that I realize how bad. *Didn't we just buy some?* I ask, my eyes flicking to see if my nipples still look sexy or if they have puffed up in resignation. *Yes,* he mutters, shifting his weight to the side. *But I used them.*

It takes a solid twenty seconds for me to realize what he means—before myself, my nipples, and my bruised ego return to a full seated position, our seatbelts fastened and tray tables up for landing. *I suppose I should have told you. I should have. But we never really determined ... We never decided what this is.* My mind flashes to the previous week when a few Biscuit fans had walked up to us and asked if I would take their photo with him. A couple others had included me in the photo as well, assuming I must be someone important if I'm walking around hand-in-hand with him. I found the photo later on the internet[22] and marveled at my eyes staring back, glassy and unrecognizable. I look over at him now, his face sheepish, and wonder just how much there is to say. No, we never clarified.

---

22. He was too cool to have his own Instagram, which left me with the not-so-casual task of sifting through fan accounts. In addition to several impressively photoshopped images of his face arranged amongst a sea of cartoon hearts and Disney characters, this search eventually revealed a dark photo where I can be seen with one arm around Biscuit, the other arm ~~signaling distress~~ waving hello to the ether, or to my waning self-worth, or to a very high number of tween girls, most of them based in Korea.

Because how can I be clear with another about what it is I need, what I want, what I *deserve*, when I—myself— have yet to determine it? If the second I seem to grasp onto a fragment of self-esteem—as soon as a beautiful man turns his lighthouse beam my way—my fingers turn to quicksand, and I mistake his confidence for my own?

I go to the bathroom, splash water on my face, and dry my hands on a $15,000 Armani suit. When I return to his bed, Biscuit is already mostly asleep; I curl up with my back to him and decide to count the slats on the window in an effort to pass time. Biscuit mumbles a question from the corner of his pillow and, ironically, in the hours that follow, proceeds to share more vulnerably, candidly, and lovingly than he has in any of the conversations we've had before. He looks at me through wet eyes and speaks to his fears, his fantasies, his blind spots, his heartbreak. I listen, knowing an invisible thorn has been pulled, and am able to be present for him—and myself—in a way that was utterly inaccessible while I still had him cast as the One Who Might Love Me. Now that I knew he wouldn't, I was free to receive whatever it was that lit us up in the first place. I grew soft to my scattered self and knew there would be a time when the attention of a beautiful man would do something other than make me a stranger to my own power, where I wouldn't sacrifice my voice, *Little Mermaid*-style, for a chance at hearing his. There would be a time when love would hit like lightning, and I would emerge louder. There would be a time—but not yet, later. Later.

~

As I write this, I have several simultaneous Google searches open; one has Biscuit's name punched in and has yielded a jumble of articles that have come out in the time since we last spoke. "Dating, Upbringing, Facts. Religion—believes in God? Y/N. Currently no confirmed relationship. Net worth?" The sidebar is littered with click bait, including "Worst Celebrity Tattoos of 2019" and "Top Celebrity Nose Jobs: Before and After." It's a strange world, and we are all doing our best to buy basic furniture in it. My brain conjures up the image of Biscuit, standing on his Los Angeles balcony, holding a mugful of instant oatmeal, musing on existential crises as improbable for him as the world makes him out to be for the rest of us.

I also remember the last drive I made to see Phantom and how my cells shook at the thought of him, but, as soon as we sat in his hotel room, the din of drunken friends and honky-tonk music around us, our faces close, I felt calm. Almost bored. The adrenaline was always conjured by the in-between, in the moments when I wasn't sure if I'd ever see him again, or the internal negotiations that said *just do it—kiss him!* The star power came from uncovering parts of myself I didn't know I had; the tiny braveries that became visible through the sheen of Hollywood sweat, lit up by the last call lights and sun that gets trapped in tall summer grasses. Celebrity or not, it took many rounds of uncertainty-poker within the world of men ("I see your ambivalence and RAISE you three hours of pretending not to notice your facial expressions!") to realize the loser, without fail, was me. And maybe *that* is the rite of passage, and maybe we do need to have the same pieces of our self-esteem obliterated over and over again to realize the indestructible parts; because at the end of the day, the ones left are the ones we need, that can breathe underwater and look better in the light than they do beneath the stars.

Today, whenever I visit Isabel, I always run my finger over the whiteboard in her kitchen where Biscuit's handwriting—spidery and faded—spells out some Shakespearean babble. He disappeared, just like Phantom did, but the pen won't. The message he wrote was meant to be romantic but has ultimately been usurped by grocery lists and, most of the time, is covered with magnets. Still, I take comfort in knowing it is there. Like anything else I needed once but has gone dormant from lack of contact. Like the reassurance that once came as a clap of thunder but now walks on tiptoes, quietly, and says in my own voice:

This. This is all mine.

Things I Like That I am Pretty Sure Make Me a Terrible Person

1. When bald people own Chihuahuas.

2. When a couple is walking down the street, one in front—mouth agape, clearly ranting—and one in back with their head bent in what I only assume is boredom. That, or they are playing a movie in their head. I like to imagine the couple is having a worse fight than I just had with my boyfriend, and therefore I am better, and will definitely find a good parking spot, because that is the law of parking spots.

3. *Full House* reruns. Do we even call them reruns anymore if all 1,000 hours are available on Netflix? How many hours did Malcolm Gladwell say it takes to be a genius at something? Anyway, in *Full House*, I am that.

4. When two people are on a first date and are not yet at the point where they can point out the other person has something green and menacing stuck between their teeth.

5. The band Kansas.

A Whole World of Left

PART ONE: JUST KIDDING

Do you ever drive behind someone going ten miles per hour
On a residential road,
One that you drive every day,
And just think, for a moment, how good it would feel
To drive as fast and as hard as you can
into the back of their car?

Me neither.

PART TWO: HERE

My grandma got hearing aids for a little while,
But the left one kept falling out,
A whole world of Left that she didn't have to hear,
While the rest of her cells jogged in place.

Certain words drop off if you don't use them, the doctor said.
The brain needs to hear them to remember
Their meaning,

And I wonder if the same thing can be said for love.
And no, not the love you feel for a landscape,
Or a baby's face as it cracks into smile,
Or even that ache in the bowl of yourself—reminding your belly that it is
Not Out of Love.

No.

I mean the type
That stands behind you with toes touching heels, arms wrapped
Into stitches,
That wakes up in the middle of the night
For fear that you'll miss something.

How long do you have to forget before it drops from the bottom of your conversation with the world,
Like the name of your first pet
Or the second word for "street?"

. . .

I sit next to my grandma,
Speaking to her right side,
And realize it has been three weeks since I've been kissed.

Three years, five months, seven hours
To the day
Since I'd spoken the underground language of love

That knows when you've finally fallen asleep
By the way that your back starts to breathe.

She turns her head toward the TV.
I turn, like a flower, toward it as well.

. . .

I ask her if she wants to hear again.
Okay, she says,
But more importantly, did you know?
This is the first time I've ever been alone

. . .

PART THREE: LISTEN

In the days leading up to it
I keep joking about how I am going to go on a date with Dev
Patel.
I read one interview in a magazine and decide that Dev and I
Would make a lovely couple.

Because he is as into the world as I am.

And living as we do,
In a time of upside down,
When the things that are never supposed to happen,
Get splashed across our TVs
It would stand to reason that
That
Which is always supposed to
Can—

So. I'm not all that surprised
When I come across the table of television stars late at night
at the Surly Goat.

And I am the one with my boots propped upon the table
With those television stars, our glasses thick with cider.
Boots that I borrowed,
And a dress made of raw silk,
That I borrowed,
Like time,
Which also hits me in all the right places
To make me feel like I'm real.

And then there is the one who tells me my gaze is Piercing,

And I almost forget to look down.

Did you know that the word Cleave,
He asks,
Means both itself and its opposite?

Makes sense, you know,
In either case it is only
Two becoming one
Or two
Again.

To cleave, to separate smoothly
And attach,
Like my tongue cleaves to the roof of my mouth
When I recall what to do with my hands.

. . .

So for the second time in my twenties, I find my legs open to
a famous person
Which is a thing that I think that I like, because they
Aren't afraid of my energy.
Still, they, like the ones who came before, are afraid of the
aftermath.
Or maybe I'm just not listening?

I have learned, now, that famous people
Who are famous for doing what they love
Just like you, only bigger,
Reminds me of what I can do,
Only bigger;
However,
Their breath on our necks
Will not make us bigger.
Their fingers don't make us more real.

And I wonder.
When will women cease to tell ourselves
To other people
As the sum of the ones who have wanted us before.
Look!
Pointing to the mounted screen-heads.
Look who made me feel real!

The pain, it seems,
Always comes from wanting more.
Not from the interviews, where he talks about his mother,
And I think how he told me
She used to make cranberry scones that would drip with butter.

Or maybe I'm just not listening.

PART FOUR: HEAR

It's the third time when
We begin talking about hearing,
And I'm listening, but also disappearing into
The way that he keeps looking away.
When you listen, he says, the goal is to hear
Just like we all look to feel seen.

Does music feel heard?
No, but it wants to be felt.
Just as I do, my back on the carpet,
George Harrison speaking in tongues.
A sentir-se,
He says in Portuguese,
And for the first time in a long time
My body remembers.

. . .

My friend says, *Don't Catch Feelings,*
Like feelings are something you catch from the bottom of a
pond
From a lack of proper footwear
Or knowing your own ground.

. . .

We walk.
Let's go this way, he says. Though I guess you came from
Over there.
Yeah, I guess it's my tendency to retrace my steps,
I reply.
And he says *it's okay,*
It's my tendency to move forward

And as we enter the doors to the grocery store,
I hear from a stranger that actually Dev Patel has just left
The canned food aisle,
Didyousee?

And to be honest, I'm not at all surprised.

Because here in the time of upside down,
When the things that are never supposed to happen—

Well.
I'm not sure what I meant when I said
That maybe because I feel too much, I'll always be alone
But I know it made sense to me once

. . .

PART FIVE: HERE

Two years later.

And it strikes me like a word that used to get lost
In the weight of what's Left,
And the people who used to drop it off when they knew I
wouldn't be home
That one day, I stopped listening for my weakness.

It was right around that exact
Right moment
That my eyes landed upon the beam of a man,
Who hurt my eyes when I looked at him straight, like squinting
Straight into the sun.

And this beam of a man, who could feel me seeing him seeing me
And how uncomfortable it made me
And how I kept having to itch at my eye
And how I would probably find ten thousand ways to get
Runny in the pan,
Before he would show me I didn't need to play broken,

Made me wonder how he could possibly hear me.

All the way down here?

But we know.

Do you know? I asked toward his face, in those early days
In the house we'd eventually share,
Letting my life fall softly upon his ear.

The same ear that my grandma tunes her body into.

And the same one that listens to me when I sometimes say

I'm afraid,

Which I say without words.

And he answers,

I know,

Again, without words.

I can tell by the way your back breathes

. . .

One day, my grandma says, I'll just forget,

And I think to myself, to forget
To forget
With an ear pressed against my thin skin,

Makes the same kind of sound as feeling it all.

I've cleaved into one

Who remembers.

Terrible Twos, Or: How a Toddler Taught me to Stop Regretting and Love the Life

1. Someone once told me we die the way we live; i.e. if you spat through life with the courtesy of a groundhog, digging shit up, you can expect the same gracelessness from death. But a sweet life begets a happy ending.

I'm not sure if I buy it. Seems to me the only "rule" in death is the fact of it. However, I do know—without fail—Benji woke up the way he fell asleep; if he went down screaming, he got up screaming. Every time. Likewise, if he sank to the mattress with his face an inch away from mine—legs and arms wrapped around my torso in total surrender, blinking a little longer each time until his eyelids eventually drooped to a close—he emerged the same way: smiling lopsidedly, shuffling his way back from whatever dream just came.

In the four months I worked as his au pair, the summer of my twenty-second year, he was almost all tenderness and limbs. He resembled a Muppet. A geyser of hair at the back of his neck, sleep running in snail trails down his pillow-pocked cheek, a soft cotton T-shirt bunched up around his belly button. I would walk out of my bedroom door to meet him, usually in my own version of sleep-dilapidation—slugs of mascara still wrecking the corners of my eyes—and do a brief assessment: is it gonna be a good day? Sometimes he would hug me around the waist, other times greet me with a hearty smack to the kneecaps. In any case, the Muppet would waddle past me down the stairs and begin his morning sonata:

"I wan ceeweal."

There are no exceptions to this rule. In life as in death, and in Benji, we come out the way we went in: wanting cereal. Maybe grumpy, maybe smiling, but with surprisingly little ailment a fresh bowl of Rice Chex can't cure.

2. The great thing about toddlers is, like dogs, they don't hold a grudge. When Benji and I would have a rough morning, or if GOD FORBID we ran out of cereal, I could count on him forgetting all about it by the time I picked him up from preschool, and certainly by the time his mom came home for dinner. If you throw a dog out on the porch because she has eaten your socks, or if you lose your temper with a two-year-old because—guess what?—he tried to eat your socks, there is usually a twenty-minute turnaround before he is ready to love you all over again.

At 3:30 p.m. every day, I would walk to meet Benji—his baby brother strapped to my chest and a string cheese sticking out of my shorts pocket—and without fail, the morning's events were irrelevant. I'd search the porch of half-pints for the one face who knew me back, for those Bambi eyes and curly head, until I found them; and when he ran out to greet me—little hands outstretched—and poured himself into my hug, it didn't matter what happened at breakfast. Grievance is a myth. We are always, always forgiven.

3. I wonder what Jimmy Choo was like as a child. Did he try on his mother's slippers, picking at the bits of fabric and lace until he knew—yes, I want to spend my life crafting horrendously beautiful women's shoes?

If so, he had nothing on Benji.

Shoes were his favorite, but fashion in general was his thing: and as for many, the source of great joy and deep frustration. We've all had those mornings when you're late for school and nothing looks good. You try on seven dresses, only to leave the house in the same jeans and t-shirt you put on when you woke up.

For Benji, this was compounded with the toddler mantra of DO IT MYSELF. It didn't matter if his buttons resembled a Rubik's cube, or if he felt the passionate need to wear a woolen sweater in ninety-degree weather: no matter what he chose—and he WOULD choose it—he insisted on putting it on himself. Getting dressed can take anywhere from five minutes to two hours; but like most things with a child, I didn't get to hit Scene Selection. I had to wait it out.

One morning at the beginning of our time together, we were on our way to catch the bus. Benji, feeling the need to change his shoes three times, sat on the floor picking at the Velcro.

Benji, we have to leave.

"NO!"

Benji, we have to go. We're going to be late.

"NO!"

Benji, we seriously need to leave . . . I'm sorry, but I am going to help you get dressed.

"NO!"

At which point he tore off his shoes, the rest of his clothing, and tried to bite my arm. With the baby in one hand and our overstuffed diaper bag in the other, I came to a crossroads:

get the child dressed and out the door through sheer force or abandon the plan altogether. Instead, I plopped down on the floor and began to bawl.

"Jenna okay? Jenna okay? Jenna crying."

Yes, Benji, I'm crying.

"Jenna crying."

Yes, Benji.

We sat there for a long time, curled into each other's arms, discussing the fact, everyone cries. He played with his toes, looking up at me every so often just to check if I had started up again; the sheer novelty of it, if nothing else, had him transfixed. I looked down at him and was wracked with guilt.

We all need our mommies sometimes, Benji, and right now I need mine.

"Jenna crying."

No, not anymore.

He looked at me and smiled. We got up hand in hand, and started to pick at the tornado of clothes on the floor; I grabbed his pants and t-shirt, and in one final valiant attempt, began to squeeze it over his head—

"DO IT MYSEEEEELLF!"

Of course.

But one way or another, eventually, he did.

4. The gift of letting a toddler "do it himself," unless you're trying to get somewhere in a hurry, is witnessing the genuine rapture of accomplishment. Doesn't matter if he pees in the toilet, drinks water out of a cup, walks down the stairs without falling, or pours a decapitated Barbie doll a cup of imaginary tea (all true): completing an action, any action, puts him on top of the world. Our walks to and from preschool were peppered with choruses of "I DIIIDDDD IITTTTT!" which certainly threw some perspective on how the rest of us approach household tasks. One morning, while making toaster waffles, I gave

it a try. The handle stayed down on the first attempt, and the waffles emerged in the most goldeny-brown way.

"I did it!!!!!"

The cats looked up at me, judging. But I was far too busy eating waffles to notice.

5. No matter the owie, no matter how big, a kiss will make it better.

6. Being around a toddler does something to our standards for basic hygiene. On a rare weekend away from Benji, I took my bone-tired ass to a local dance festival, simply for the experience of being around other adults doing adult things.[23] My bar was already low. I felt it dip even further after each day on the dance floor; tiptoe-stumbling back to my tent, caked in a sheen of sweat and a layer of Oregon mud, I fell asleep on the forest duff without so much as a thought of a toothbrush. Disgusting? Maybe. But like I said, my bar was low.

Before Benji was enrolled in a half-day preschool program, it was a miracle if I had time to put on clean underwear, let alone shower or do something to my hair to make it resemble anything other than roadkill. Once he began leaving in the mornings, I eventually got the chance to hop in the shower — but learned quickly I couldn't expect the clean to last longer than an hour or two.

I'd hold Benji's baby brother in my arms, obsessed with his inability to sprint away from me. But then, spit up happened. Often more than once in the space of five minutes. Creamed carrots happened, close-range urinations happened, and applesauce explosions happened... usually on my way out the door.

I gave up on the idea of cleanliness because other things mattered more.

---

23. When does one feel like an adult? I don't know, but I assume it has something to do with taxes?

One afternoon as I lay comatose on my bed, staring at the ceiling and contemplating which future-building career nonsense I wanted to procrastinate on first, Benji did a nose-dive onto my stomach.

OOF.

He hauled himself onto my torso, planting one knee on either side, and grinned the biggest grin that has ever been grinned.

"Jenna, I LOVE you."

And happiness swam through my body like electricity. There is no feeling like it. None.

Benji, I love you so much. You're my best boy.

At which point Benji's smile cracked open, his eyes lit up, and he delivered a stream of saliva directly into my open mouth.

I leapt up, running to the bathroom in a futile attempt at disinfection, knowing if I had to choose between a clean mouth and hearing someone say he loves me—his crinkly eyes revealing the way he really, truly, loves me, for the silly parts of myself I rarely allowed grown-ups to see—I'd choose the latter. Every time.

7. Have you ever heard "The Wheels on the Bus Go Round and Round?" How about the lesser-known verses, like the mommies on the bus (shh shh shh) and the money on the bus (clink clink clink) and the horn on the bus (beep beep beep)? Have you ever heard it more than once in the same day? How about twenty-seven times?

I have.

8. Benji's mother, at the time of our contract, was training to be a Montessori teacher. If I learned anything from proximity, it's the way most two-year-olds hate to be uprooted. They get off on an inner mechanism of order; the pink spoon goes in the pink spoon spot, we wash our hands after we use the potty, we hold hands when we cross the street. So what happens when

you uproot a toddler not one, not two, but three times over the course of one summer?

In a word: poop. When the world as they know it appears to be crashing down, when they can't get a grip on where or when they are supposed to sleep, some kids take to exercising autonomy over the one thing they can control—their bowels. And by some kids, I mean Benji. All in all, he did incredibly well; he traveled overseas from Thailand,[24] crashed in a disastrous Airbnb, and then moved through two separate houses in Eastern Portland before leaving again for the year. And in all the backing and forthing, there was only one incident where he felt the need to smear feces on the shower curtain.

What started out as sheer disgust from me, though, morphed over time into empathy; what would I do, for example, if I were in his miniature shoes? What did I do when I was just a little bit older than he was, packing up my little blue suitcase twice a week to volley back and forth between my parents?

I remember sitting in the counselor's office at Roosevelt Elementary, mandatory penance for any kid dealing with Divorce. Divorce. It had such a dull clang to it, even then; but all I really remember feeling was annoyance at the counselor's inability to anticipate my game preference. I mean, Checkers? Really? I was five. She could have at least invested in some Disney gear. Instead, we bookended each other once a week—the counselor and I—around a checkerboard and a state-funded program, neither one adequately stacked to handle what might unfold.

Since then, I've continued to uproot. The period leading up to my au pair gig was spent overseas; people constantly

---

24. When I reflect upon the fact that Benji's mom made the trip ALONE with two babies and no Netflix, I want to cry in shame for how little I knew about how to support her, or any mom for that matter. I kept her children safe and loved, which was enough—and still, I could have acknowledged her more. Perhaps no one really gets it, until we are in it ourselves; but once we know, we can never forget. So: the next time you see a mother alone on a plane with screaming babies, kindly offer her your indentured servitude, a bucket-sized martini, and a cool $10k. I think that oughta do it.

asked me if I missed my own bed, and sure, I might have. I missed the idea. But the truth is, my early twenties were marked by a sudden death in the feeling of my "own bed," or the comfort such an idea had contained before. And even then, I had a suspicion that home is something we create. It's not a mattress.

So. One sticky July evening, his mom and I took Benji out for ice cream at Salt and Straw, a Portland mecca. After waiting in line with two small children for over an hour,[25] we settled at a table near the corner; about five minutes into devouring, I pressed too hard on the side of my cone, and it inexplicably shattered. The sacrificial ice cream wasn't even Benji's; but somehow, in his brain, it didn't matter. Something about seeing the cone explode into dozens of sugary pieces, no longer the shape it arrived in, set off an alarm in his head.

Fat tears rolled down his face, and as we cooed over his banshee level scream—half-entertained, half-stunned at his devastation over something seemingly trivial—I began to think. We all crave a sense of order. For me, at the time, it didn't mean staying in one place; if anything, it was irregularity I sought out, and would for some time. But even irregularity was a pattern. I can drink my coffee in a different kitchen every two weeks, but you can be damn sure it's coffee I'll be drinking.

9. Shameless perk of hanging out with a toddler: access to your own personal parrot. In one day, I would get Benji to tell a stranger he is a "Classy Gentleman," could ask him to say "HELLOOOOO LADY!" to the representative assisting me from Virgin America, and could trick him into rattling off a series of toddler tongue-twisters like Perplexing. Or Transylvania. Or Crisps.

"Pedrprexeen. Dansyrvendah. Kips."

---

25. AND THE NOBEL PEACE PRIZE GOES TO

I'd swear to use my powers for good and not evil. But the next time the bus driver sighed audibly when I struggle to collapse the un-collapsable stroller, he had another thing coming.

"HELLOOOO, baaathead."

10. He certainly gave no shits about it—and at times, I forgot it myself—but I did have a life outside of my time with Benji. Entering into his space each day was like entering the wardrobe of *Narnia*; the outside world did not cease to exist, but I found it hard to focus on any of its details while his tiny hand was clasped within mine.

Then, one day the parallel universe of twentysomething life opened up and revealed sharp teeth: a phone call, and news that my not-quite-ex—who felt like much more than "boyfriend"— had been arrested. He hadn't overdosed. He'd been arrested. He wasn't dead. He was in trouble. But until I heard the news and noticed my breath catch, I didn't realize how on edge I'd been—how I always knew it was going to be one or the other.

I remember exactly where I was standing; the sound of pad thai sizzling on the stovetop, the exact weight of the pink skirt hanging from my hips as the voice continued: *He's going away. It's like the military. You aren't going to see him anymore.*

Half my brain thought:

I won't make it.

The other half thought:

At last. I'm free.

The contrast left my brain feeling sunburnt; but not long afterward, the control center switched over to Numb. I gave up trying to understand. I ate the pad thai, but my throat closed around it.

The worst part, perhaps, about caring for an addict is knowing you are powerless. Nothing you can say or do will alleviate the fact that they are at war with themselves. My hopelessness was a defense mechanism, but at least it was mine.

Meanwhile, the door to Benji *Narnia* re-opened, 7:00 a.m. on the dot, just as it always did. The Numbness listened to toddler Pandora and tried to perfect the ratio of almond butter to raspberry jelly. The Numbness did my laundry, went jogging, and even spent time with friends; it inhabited a functioning body, kept it functioning, but did nothing to bring light into the places where hopelessness took up residence and started doing the crossword.

Benji was the light. It took some time, but eventually, his unwavering hope—his unflinching belief in every day as the BEST DAY EVER because he gets to eat CEREAL—shuttled me back into optimism. Like animals, toddlers can smell fear, and I swear they can smell sadness, too; and for the week I needed him most, Benji enveloped me in love without asking for anything in return. (Except maybe an almond butter and raspberry jelly sandwich. Or two. Or three.)

We walked to the lip of the wardrobe. We stepped over.

11. Forget what you've heard about the Terrible Twos. Nothing you've ever seen on television, no half-guilty glance at the mom in the supermarket dragging her kid by the snap on his overalls, could possibly sum up what it is actually like to deal with a toddler at peak tantrum unless you've lived through it.

Benji, despite all his warmth and gooey goodness, took toddlerhood very seriously, and was capable of taking his voice into a realm that would make Gollum from *Lord of the Rings* say, "Geez, take it down a notch." A scream so potent, you're left wondering if it's even human.

It rendered me inert. My limbs went still like a stunned chicken. And the worst part was the unpredictability; it almost never emerged in relation to anything substantial. If he actually faceplanted on the sidewalk, more often than not, he would shake it off and keep running. Brushing teeth, however, was an all-out war.

"I WANNA BRUSH MY TEEEEEEETH!!!!!!!"

Benji, when you throw your toothbrush in the toilet, you don't get to brush your teeth.

"WANNA BRUUUSHH TEEEEEEEEEETH."

Benji, I don't like it when you punch me in the neck.

And so it went. This was usually the point where the baby cried, inspired by the general cacophony and not one to be outdone by flying toothbrushes.

Sometimes, I would smell the tantrum coming a mile away; like when we were about to cross the street and Benji would give me this look, like "I am going to do anything and everything in my power to scare the living bejeezus out of you." At this point, he would catapult across the street in a flash of sandals and hair, forcing me to pin him to the sidewalk and wrestle him into the stroller, where he proceeded to scream himself into oblivion. I usually walked around the block a few times, smiling eerily at anyone who passed by, pretending I—like they—had no idea how this demon snuck into my stroller.

When he finished howling, however, Benji would bring his hands up to his face and begin his mantra. "Takea deeep breat, caaaam down. Takea deeep breat, caaam down." He would do it for five minutes sometimes before needing a response.

That's right, Benji. Deep breaths.

"Big hug, Jenna."

Big hug, Benji.

At one point in our time together, a lightbulb went off. He was, quite apparently, in his terrible twos—throwing fits in grocery stores because he was tired, or they moved the yogurt-covered raisins, or he had forgotten what his voice sounds like, or whatever—so where was I? When I began nannying for him, I was twenty-two years old. TWICE the two, 2x the terrible, 2x the need to throw tantrums at bath time. I proposed this idea to Benji once, watching dazedly as he constructed a tower of legos. What do you think about that, Benji?

"Peanutbuddur petzels."

So we really weren't so different, him and I. No wonder we found each other. All we ever wanted, all we were ever truly screaming for, were peanut butter pretzels and a decent nap.

12. When you're a child, there's this delicious feeling of riding in the back of a vehicle and losing all sense of time and space. It doesn't matter where you are, or where you're going; all you know is you're getting there, and someone else is making sure you do.

You can close your eyes, the sounds of the street ebbing as your consciousness does. There's no resistance in this. No wondering whether you should take out your contacts before you fall asleep, no fretting over whether you've shut down your computer or fed your fish or finished the shit standing between you and a good night's sleep.

Benji, one day and one foot in front of the other, inspired me to feel joy down to my skinny skin skin. I remember driving with him to Sauvie Island. Watching as he ran into the water—feet galloping over one another, his perfect baby skin glowing under tiny droplets of sun and sea. Something like wonder awakened within me. It felt both discovered and remembered.

Before I met Benji, I had forgotten. Forgotten, until I watched him eat hummus by the fistful, bits of cracker stuck in his hair, blackberries staining his cheeks and chin. Forgotten until he would run into my lap, wrapping his arms around my neck and pressing his nose to mine; giving me a look to say he'd trust me forever, his accordion ribcage crumpling and expanding like it's just learned how to breathe.

I wrote in my journal. *Benji.*

When I think of leaving you, I want to collapse.

13. To walk down the street with a toddler is to know you might end up staring at the same flower for twenty minutes, and often do.

14. The roof of my mouth has already healed from where I burned it on my pizza. I run my tongue over its slickness and understand: Our hearts have the ability to mend themselves. Isn't it amazing how things fade?

Some things, however, stay with us.

As my summer with Benji came to a close, my brain would often pitch forward to years down the road, picturing him as an adult—running down the street, or through the forest, toward or away from something, everything—and hoped we would both retain what his toddlerhood taught me. It's been years, but I remember the exact way he would sprint toward the swing set, or into my arms at the end of the school day; how he'd collapse into bed, blanket tucked under his arm, sleep already saturating the pillow before his eyes even closed. He had no regrets. None. He surged through life like a rocket, knowing each day is NEW, and better than the last—how could it not be? Sure, one day we got to watch The Elephant Show, but the next day, we'd probably do it again. And again. And again.

Being around Benji planted seeds of self-confidence which took a decade to bloom; but somehow, and with enough attention, they did.

Often after finding myself tangled, focusing on a dude instead of on what my heart desired, I'd come back to the memory of how I felt whilst in charge of this little, magic human. Any time I was told I was "too much," I'd remember Benji screaming at the top of his lungs whilst standing atop a dining room table, pantsless, covered in glitter glue. Something would glue back together inside me as well.

A boyfriend who became an addict was not the defining failure of my maturity. Nor was a night with a beautiful, shiny man at a music festival the pinnacle of my womanhood. A highlight, sure—but not the pinnacle. This is the lesson I was left with, after Benji: life, if we choose to see it as so, is really only ever getting better all the time. There's always a bigger playground, better shoes, more mercy with ourselves, more joy than we thought we were capable of.

Benji, he wanted to grow up. He was in a hurry to get to those shoes. I wonder all the time whether he is happy, now he surely has them.

And me? I'm still fitting into mine, but they get comfier—and more like something a toddler would wear? Is Velcro uncool?—all the time. I'm learning to be content where I am: sitting in the dining room in a house I have filled with flowers and off-brand cereal, cup of tea at my elbow. I have new appreciation for the type of freedom I've earned with time; the kind which comes with having suffered, experienced, lived.

Benji didn't know that type of freedom—neither one of us could, in our terrible twos. But we did know, and he reminded me, what it meant to move from the heart. He did it every day without trying. It was as natural to him as a swing set, or opening his mouth to taste a rainstorm. The puddles lined the sidewalk, and we held hands, and we jumped. Looking both ways as we crossed the street, and into the sweetness of life.

Far Out

J don't know if you've noticed, but there are babies in the air. Babies, flying around like bits of cotton, like ideas which get stuck in your teeth or to the bottom side of a pillow that's been folded into a featherbed. The air is colder now, and we've added more layers. I feel, in the blue of the morning, a warming inside of my body like honey being dripped from the sky. A sky full of babies. Babies who are wanted, not wanted, always wanted, but without a place to land—soft, like a featherbed—and dozens of reasons why now is not the time.

The girl in the booth next to me says, "Maybe in ten years—but I mean, it'll be an adjustment. I mean, I want that," and I picture her baby in a red and white hat, frowning into a pile of chins. Because it, like all the others, knows it is needed—right here, right now—but that doesn't mean anything is going to be easy. That doesn't mean we're going to smile for every smartphone. That doesn't mean there is time to waste on things like arguing with the wait staff, or texting on the toilet, or a random person doubling back to tell me this is a table for *two*—not for three.

I crouch here now, at the booth where no one is watching, pretending to be concerned about the table for two-not-three. Scribbling this down when I should be clearing wine glasses, because I must, because there are babies in the air—and there are words pouring out of me like a thing which must be born. It must leave my body so it can be a body once more rather than this, a receptacle for potential, because you never really know which thing will be the one to save us.

It doesn't have to be a *human* baby. For me, right now, it's words. Ideas. Dances. Vegetable soups. But that doesn't mean I don't walk in this body, suddenly awake and didn't wait in line at the pharmacy, feeling my belly light up with potential and then dim again, like a coal mistaking footsteps for fire. I didn't ask it to wake up. Then again, maybe none of us do—ask to wake up—we just do, and we talk about it on hikes with our friends the way suddenly, what once was outer space, now feels like a guest house.

And a whole bunch of babies, flying through the air, texting their real estate agents because—*this*. This is the time to buy.

Like the two women at work, who announce their pregnancies at the same staff meeting and the third who says she's adopting. I watch what they eat, an anthropologist of what it takes to grow life, fascinated by trail mix and small bits of noodle and the subtle difference between one person saying, "I'm pregnant," and the other saying, "we're pregnant." Because she said *we*, and the room shifted in its shoes. Shifted its body position, the exact fold of its arms, to be able to hold what was now—subconsciously—our collective responsibility: *we*.

Maybe it's because the world feels like it's crumbling. Maybe because, as it does, it feels like we are growing up. Maybe because those two have never been separate: birth, death, and all the goo in between making us want to be better than the ones who came before.

Like the friend who announced her pregnancy the same week her husband was (very publicly) accused of assaulting a girl at our old school. Both he and his brother and their friend—the one who always wore gel in his hair and put the word "personal" in parentheses on his Facebook page, because he and his actions take up two different plots in space—all three of them mistaking apathy for consent, youth for hunger, time for healing. The sucker punch of this news hit in my womb, made me go, *No! Not a world like this. How does someone move on in a world like this? Feel safe in a world like this? Bring life into a world like this?* Back to that kind of life, the one existing outside of this page. The kind of life which asks for breath, and food, and eventually the car keys, and eventually permission to say: I forgive you.

I asked myself permission to say I forgive you. To the person who assaulted his friend—though I didn't know it then—five years before he looked at me, full body facing mine, as I sat on the hood of his car, saying, *I trust you.* Let's make something.

Let's birth a project in the world where once there was none.

And now, there's just one: a singular, barbed-wire thought, *just what will it take to make a world where this isn't so?*

Just how far out into the middle of the road do we have to go for a girl to walk home in the middle of the night and not dwell on the footsteps behind her? To scan the internet and not find one single word about blacking out at a party; piecing together the story of the night by the pieces of clothing which don't quite line up, aren't quite where she left them, wasn't quite what she planned.

When I was fresh out of college, older men were the only ones who hit on me. Typically, ones who were somehow both balding AND had ponytails reaching their middle backs, who waited until my dad was far enough out of earshot to make a comment about my shirt; not much, but enough so I forgot I was the one underneath it. Meanwhile, I was ignored by the boys my age and locked myself into the paradox of not wanting to be objectified and yet pained, somehow, at the invisibility of not being *wanted.* At least, not by anyone who could write it down in my yearbook, birth it, make it real: *I see you.* It didn't matter if I was the one they were seeing.

I feel my breath catch now, when I listen to young women tell me they *hate* when people catcall them at the bus stop.... "Hey, baby, you want a ride? You don't need to take that bus. *Y O U* don't need to take that bus." ... but who then wonder, when they are passed by, if it means they are ugly. Undesirable. The worth living underneath the shirt; do not pass GO; do not collect $200. Do not come back for anything. Least of all, what they told you—once—you could be.

We all get born differently. For me, the change happened when I finally went out—out far—out way, way far, past the line of bamboo stalks and the electric, purple-gray sky. Past the point where I could feel my feet, cracked and dusty, in the middle of an Oregon field. Past the initial full-body chill of not knowing which way I had come from and leaning instead into the veins of a redwood tree: open, breathing. It was only when I found myself in nature, alone, that the paradox finally broke. Alone. Together. Dying. Alive. Wanting nothing, wanted by everything. The way rocks feel cold to the touch and are a thousand miles deep—and the way birds shuffle into place when they know you aren't leaving. I healed in those spaces. I felt it shift, like life shifts inside of a womb: little foot scraping along the walls of a world it already knows will expand.

I listen to the women at the booth next to mine. I recognize one from high school, a senior when I was a freshman, and immediately hide my face. I mean—she's a *senior.* They are talking about things like babies and migraines and listing the names of medications which sound like rejected Disney villains: *Cymcrocrimptin. Vallsniak. Cellbrohnzan.* They might as well be speaking an alien tongue. Then there's me, wearing tie-dye socks with holes in the bottom, still uncertain of how to do taxes even after doing them ten times. The information enters my brain each April, and then flies straight into the sun by May. Still. And then there's the words they speak—*Hallboneethin, Cymotrol,* "good school district"— and I'm about as far out as a football field. I'm lost on their ears, even if I could yell, "Hey—I'm a body too! Am I allowed to have this feeling inside of me? Can I carry a house that one day builds life? Can I do it without getting a credit card??"

Right now, I'm at yet another in-between. The awareness something is coming, but the not-quite-there-yet. In the meantime, I listen to all that still wants to be life and watch it slip through the fingers of my sisters as they braid strips of leather; braid hair; braid stories together until there's nothing left but love. Letting love slip through my fingers as I crouch inside this booth, lest it slip through the cracks of forever. It's true: *We* are pregnant—all of us here; the red and striped hats; the nights spent alone; the parallel parking. We are creating something new. Is it so far out to consider it might be something good?

It occurs to me, suddenly—sitting here with my holey socks and lack of financial literacy, with my neediness and greatness and all the times I've eaten peanut butter cups from the bulk food bins and all the times I even felt *good* about it—I love my life. And the thought, one simple thought, is the single most far-out idea that has ever, EVER, passed through my brain. For a time, it would have been a foreign tongue; and now it is clear, tiny yet clear, like a bell in the night.

Like these fingers, picking babies from the air. Threading stories. Wanting nothing.

Like my heart, and spilling secrets. Like this body. Waking up.

Closure:
We Have What We Need

Or at least, almost. There could always be more snacks.

How are you?
Did we deliver on our promises?
All of us?

I think it's normal to feel stunned, and a little puzzled, when parts of ourselves get reflected back—moon on the water, ripples casting the image out into fractals of light—when they are familiar, but also not quite.

How can that be the moon down there, when it's all the way up in the sky?

I remember the first time I saw my child's face on an ultrasound. It was one of the creepy 3D ones I'm pretty sure I declined, but they did it anyway, because the tech was bored, and it was almost lunch. I peered at the screen, and there it was. I was stunned, and a little puzzled.

He has my chin.

How can that be when I'm right here, right in front of my own face?

I Was Told I'd Be Glowing

*T*his is about America. Rather, it is about knowing exactly what you want, getting it, then losing your shit (because it doesn't feel anything like you thought it would), and tunneling into your couch for four months watching *The Bachelor*. If that's not American, I don't know what is.

(Except maybe the tiny, resilient, dead-of-night instinct to make sense of it all, to believe the revolution you'd hoped for wasn't the one you expected but might be the one you needed. That is American too.)

I'll explain.

On March 31, 2020, eighteen days after COVID-19 was named a public emergency, I found out I am pregnant. I had just peeled the pink, sateen duvet off the bed I shared with my boyfriend; it was a paisley monstrosity my mother had loaned us, and I never liked it, but still stared at it for thirty days while the world decimated outside our window. Then, on March 31 — after returning home with a vat of hand sanitizer, packet of new sponges for my grandma, and home pregnancy test — I finally freed our bed from its silky prison and marched straight into the bathroom to pee on a stick. Earlier in the day, when I mentioned my period was late but probably delayed as a result of the apocalypse, my boyfriend's eyes had rocketed into his forehead.

"Can you imagine if you were pregnant? *That* would be *nuts.*" Fast forward a few hours: the stick blinked back at us with double pink lines, and the only thing I could think about was the fact we had conceived our first child on the ugliest duvet I'd ever seen in my life. In the middle of a pandemic.

We woke up the next morning, April Fool's Day, and cried.

Note: there are occasions in life when panic is a warranted response. One is the outbreak of a deadly virus. Another is awakening to the systemic racism you've steeped in since birth. Another yet is realizing the two are happening simultaneously while, at the *same* time, being faced with bringing another *brand new human* into a world that prepared you to post about babies on Instagram but had done nothing to normalize the icy dread spidering through your veins.

As I hugged the bathroom floor during those first days, I recalled every movie in which a woman realizes her Life's Greatest Potential upon discovering she's pregnant and never has a bad day again. She is the same person who announces it while dining at a French restaurant, pulling a red napkin off her husband's plate to reveal a positive pregnancy test beneath. They both begin to laugh-cry, oblivious to the fact this woman has essentially urinated onto the table, and probably revisit all their wedding photos that night in bed. She will throw up exactly once in a subsequent scene. Approximately four minutes later, she is featured with her hair tied up in a silk scarf, painting a nursery while her watermelon belly swells beneath a Ralph Lauren polo. She has already gone jogging. On one swift brushstroke, her water will break with gusto onto the hardwood floor; in the next image, she has a delightfully pink infant cradled in her arms, who is likely portrayed by a five-month-old child actor who no longer looks like a swamp creature and already has his SAG card.

This scene, the only one I'd been reliably exposed to, conveys two resounding messages: One, that delight is the only response to conceiving a baby. Two, that women are supposed to carry a baby while carrying on with life as normal—wear mascara, exercise, and get shit done. No one ever told me confusion, shock, and ambivalence are perfectly normal—nay, healthy—responses to pregnancy, as to a pandemic. It is as futile to expect all pregnant women to be overjoyed as it is to expect all quarantined adults to develop an expert recipe for banana bread, thriving yoga practice, and robust sex life as a result of being trapped at home.

So even though I felt excitement beneath the confusion, like a fleck of gold visible in a creek bed, I also judged the turmoil fuming inside my body. I was afraid to admit I felt less than certain: mortified to have gotten what I had wanted, had quietly prayed for, and still wasn't ready for. For weeks, I tunneled into comparison with others and sunk into the cryptic advice strangers—most of them male—felt entitled to share.

"You women are so *anxious*," an uncle slurred one night, plonking down the beer he had also instructed me not to drink. The manifest destiny of mansplainers everywhere rested on his boozy shoulders.

"You should just *enjoy* this experience. It's the best time of your life. Enjoy it."

And in that moment, something clicked: I was overcome with the urge to ask if *he* was enjoying it. The "it" being his very own pregnancy: the conception, gestation, and painful birth humanity seemed to be experiencing during the dumpster fire of 2020. I got it. Beneath his idiotic comment rested a crucial idea: maybe, just maybe, the challenge-yet-hope-yet-denial-yet-glory which defined my early pregnancy was a mirror of the global conundrum. Here we were, faced with the opportunity to re-evaluate everything leading up to this point—inequity, healthcare, productivity, our parents' testy relationship—and we, all of us, balked at the task. The world burned and still wanted to go to brunch. I was growing a strawberry-sized human inside my uterus and still wanted to organize the garage. In between meetings. Our resistance was catching up to us.

Luckily, the same spirit who chose this godforsaken year to make his entrance had little tolerance for my ego, nor for my lifelong habit of Caring What Other People Think. Cue "Puke Fest 2020": just as my head wrapped around the reality of birth, my stomach began turning itself inside out with the subtlety of a chainsaw, all day every day. And I was *shocked.* The same part of me who assumed I'd feel elation at pregnancy also assumed I would adore the bodily changes that came with it. I was certain I would feel like a celebrity, round and magical, with a mane of hormonally juiced hair. I was told I'd be glowing but, instead, felt as if I were back on the boat in Lake Havasu, hungover, after being hit on the head with a blunt object.[26] Twenty-four hours a day. The smell of my own skin, the taste of my own mouth, the inkling someone within a fourteen-block radius might be cooking bacon—all were fodder for the kind of demonic vomiting I'd only seen before in movies. And not the ones about babies.

I became the kind of sick people don't want to talk about.

Anyone who has ever cleared a room with the word "tampon" can understand incessant puking—coupled with a torn esophagus and lack of basic hygiene—falls outside the microscopic window of tolerance socially allotted for women's health issues. When it comes to "morning" sickness, we are trained to believe it should be gone by the second trimester. Well-meaning friends bring crackers and packets of ginger candies for a few weeks but, by the time the fourth month

---

26. Hindsight is 20/20. Or is 2020 hindsight? I gained a new empathy for the women at that fucking bachelorette party, for their inflatable penises and questionable BBQ tactics, after joining their ranks as a parent-to-be. They weren't psychopaths. They were new mothers. They deserved a break. Let them eat soggy cake.

arrives, you better be ready for them to shift to baby shoes and blatant judgments about breastfeeding plans. Well into month six, I was still flinging open the car door to vomit into parking lots, making watery eye contact with horrified passersby who seemed to need to hear "I'm pregnant" in order to survive the ordeal of seeing me. On more than one occasion, I experienced the distinct glare of *where's your bump, then, bitch* as a deli customer realized she should probably move her Tesla out of the splatter zone. When my boyfriend would return to the car with sixteen cases of sparkling water and a packet of pretzels, I could only look up at him in a tired combination of love, appreciation, and total resentment at his ability to operate a motor vehicle.

"What did *I* do," he would sometimes ask, peering around the doorjamb as I yelled in helpless, illogical rage.

"Nothing," I'd answer. "I'm just mad at you for existing so easily."

It took me five months of near-constant vomiting to consider—perhaps—my body was having a reasonable response to the events transpiring outside. The murder of George Floyd dominated the news, bringing the reality of racist America inescapably forward, and I threw up. College students partied on yachts in Florida, none of them wearing masks, and I threw up. My home state of California burned to a crisp as the air quality index crept beyond the four hundred point all over the west coast, and I threw up. I called friends, senators, and grandparents to ask for forgiveness, for justice, and for tools to move forward.

"I'm just tired," a friend told me, reflecting on her experience as a Black woman in America. "I'm so tired, and mad. Others can just exist so easily. I . . . can't."

And I threw up.

Meanwhile, life continued.

Ruth Bader Ginsberg began her last months on Earth, the bougainvillea plant began blooming outside my front window, and I grew a pancreas, liver, heart, brain, and teeny set of lungs inside my belly. All while surviving on sourdough toast. On one of my better days, I met my friend Bryce for a walk at the beach. He, like the wise man he is, greeted me with a cold juice and ample distance. I remember the way the salt air sank into my skin, both stinging and nourishing my largest and most visible organ.

"I didn't expect to feel so exposed," I told him, outrage and gratitude continuing their infinite cha-cha inside my psyche. "It's like whatever layer I had left has been stripped away. I feel the suffering of others like a virus. Pregnancy—this change—has turned me inside out. And I worry I won't ever go back."

"Well," he paused, looking out at the sea. As I mentioned, this is a wise man. He often looks to large bodies of water for clues. "I don't think you will. I mean, none of us will. This year has taken away the illusion that everything is okay, and it's painful. But it's left us with something else—the truth. It's like your pregnancy. America is also gestating something new—something that can, one day, be better—but in the meantime, our current body is rejecting it. Just like yours is registering your baby as a foreign entity. We are all being tasked to let something grow that was always part of our potential . . . but in order to let it grow, we have to let go of the old part."

He paused. "We have to shut up and let the future in."

We walked for hours that day, seeking patches of shade. I ate saltine crackers from my pocket and tried to find comfortable positions to sit in, and, eventually, I gave up. Comfort is nice, but it's not part of my life right now. Or anyone's.

Today, my baby is almost ready to come out of my body and into the world. With each passing moment, I feel like I know him more . . . and also not at all. Having children is the ultimate mystery; you know there's a chance they will have your eyes or his hair texture, but the personality is invariably up for grabs. Ask any parent who has spent thirteen hours reading the *Captain Underpants* series out loud to a group of spiky-headed extroverts. Confusion is normal.

As for me: over time, the uncertainty I began this revolution with has made way for something resembling peace. Creeping from its supernatural, Loch Ness depth has come the knowing I asked for—and needed—all along: this exact baby, this exact time, this exact challenge. My initial lack of recognition was an integral part of losing myself in order to show up for something better which, I hope, deep in my core, everyone will. That there will come a time when we look into the eyes of this thing we have made, all of us, and know we have welcomed it.

Maybe we needed the puking phase to get here.

Meanwhile, the labor—not to mention parenting, the real work—still lies ahead.

At one point—nearing what would be the end of Pukefest, though I didn't know it at the time—I was standing in line to enter Whole Foods, complying with COVID-19 capacity restrictions, when a man walked up behind me. I recognized his face, but not really, in a way that often happens to me while adulting in my hometown.

Someone my parents knew. A childhood friend's father. Someone, who—at one point—I believed to have total authority over me. If his daughter had hosted a sleepover, he would have made us waffles in the morning and I would have eaten them without question. Later, if he had said we needed to be home by ten, I would have believed him. If he had punished us for sneaking out, I would have borne it in silence. Even later, if he had told me what career I should explore, or who to date, or who to become, I would have listened. Even if I didn't want to, I would have cared.

But looking at him as an adult, I saw he was all those things and nothing to me. In the way every single one of us is a mishmash of every identity which has come before. He was—we are, each of us—a collection of all our moons.

The same man who had once told me my music taste was "a little intense" now stood in front of me, hair thinning, in a Jimmy Buffett t-shirt and a muted expression that, despite his best effort, could not hide his anxiety. I felt something tender for him, and for myself. I wanted to know what he had to say, not because of his paternal power over me, but because he was another human—and humans, despite their best efforts, continue to win me over.

I am growing into a whole new person, and growing another person, too. I could feel him moving inside my belly, the size of a cantaloupe; I could sense all the phases he still has ahead, the way his hand will one day outgrow mine, the new kind of man he'll be tasked to become. I imagined the role I'll play; the ways I'll be able to influence him, and the ways I never can. The way he just wants, floating around in there, to be given the chance. The chance to learn.

I looked at the man in front of me. I wanted to hear what he had to say. But, finally—gorgeously— I didn't *need* to.

He absorbed my dilapidated wave with timid eyes before looking down at my belly; we made chitchat about my parents, the weather, the infernos, the Emmys. He asked, "How are you handling pregnancy?"

As I stood there, silently preparing for the inevitable barrage of advice on how to treat hemorrhoids, I smiled to myself; he was trying his best. Ready to make waffles. I considered changing the subject. Had he seen the news today? If so, how is he feeling? Who is he becoming, given all that is breaking?

Breathe breathe breathe, push, push, push.

He glanced up then, seeing it was almost my turn to cross the threshold, and paused. "It's good to see you. You look ... um ..."

"I know, I know." My greasy hair was stacked on top of my head, and I'm pretty sure my glasses were taped. My shirt was stained with old Pepsi, because it was still the only beverage I could keep down, and my chin was peppered with angry, hormonal acne. I hadn't showered in days. I looked up at him, with a smile that was somewhere between—or perhaps an amalgamation of—a middle finger and genuine overflow of love. I saw myself clearly now. I didn't need him to.

"I know. Totally radiant. And with any luck, we'll all get through it together."

Other People I Can Thank

1. All the men who "wronged" me
2. My mother
3. Myself
4. All of it, all of us. All phases. All ways.

Acknowledgments

I am forever indebted to the writers who have come before me; namely, the women brave enough to share stories on their own terms, whose words changed my life. This list includes, but is not limited to: Adrienne Rich, Ann Lamott, Jessi Klein, Sheila Heti, Samantha Irby, Miranda July, Anne Carson, Ann Patchett, and Lucy Grealy. Thank you to the mentors who supported me in finding my voice and running with it, especially Patty Ruth, Emily Cuming, and Jill Littlewood. Thank you to Tony Sandrich, the first teacher to tell me to keep writing, and then wouldn't shut up about it.

This book would not exist without the steadfast support of Yvette Keller, who came into my life like some sort of miracle, and helped identify the through line of this work with enormous dedication and warmth. Thank you to Rachael Quisel for taking deep care with the copy edit, modeling both precision and sensitivity, and to the entire team at She Writes Press for taking a chance on a collection that does not fall into a singular genre. Thank you to Marissa DeCuir and the team at Books Forward for demonstrating a remarkable cross section of excitement and professionalism in promoting this work.

Thank you to the staff at Handlebar Coffee and Yellow Belly Taproom for allowing me to sit and work on this project well past closing time.

Shout out to my family, especially my parents and in-laws, for not disowning me after reading some of these essays. Gratitude to my mother, who gifted me with the daisy chain. Gratitude to my father, who taught me that being a good person is just as important as being a good artist, and told me one million times to prioritize my own interests over chasing boys. The content of this book is proof that I ignored him, and the publishing of it is proof that I eventually listened. Thank you both for giving me life and making me sandwiches even when I probably should have made them myself.

Thank you, Nicholas and Felix, who are the backbone of my life, for your unwavering love and patience. Nicholas: the man you are makes me excited to raise children together. Parenting with you is my greatest dream come true, and the life we have built was worth every bump in the road.

Lastly, thank you to the bumps in the road. Thank you to each challenging relationship, each broken trust, each comical blunder. You are my teachers, and I have learned to navigate the world and love myself in part through your lessons. I wouldn't trade a thing.

About the Author

*J*enna Tico survived the best years of her life by incessantly journaling, scribbling poetry, and distracting herself from her questionable choices with potato chips and excellent friendships. Now in her mid-thirties, she is a community-builder, performing artist, wife, mother, writer, and group facilitator. Jenna lives with her family in Santa Barbara, CA.

Author photo © Lerina Winter

Looking for your next great read?

We can help!

Visit www.shewritespress.com/next-read
or scan the QR code below for a list
of our recommended titles.

She Writes Press is an award-winning
independent publishing company founded to
serve women writers everywhere.

Printed in the USA
CPSIA information can be obtained
at www.ICGtesting.com
CBHW030211090424
6601CB00003B/11

2 370001 859081

Cancer
Moon